"Accessible, winsome, and rooted in on-the-ground experience, this book does nothing less than sketch out an entire 'theatrical ecosystem' informed by a vibrant scriptural imagination. A must-read for all who seek a generous vision for what has been a much-neglected art in the current theology and arts conversation."

—JEREMY BEGBIE
Duke University

"I am thrilled this extraordinary resource exists. *The Problem with the Dot* is historical, futuristic, and theologically cogent. Most importantly to me, an actor in NYC, this book is creatively practical. It is a balm of affirmation to anyone who feels called to the theater and called to Christian faithfulness. It is also a loving challenge to those who have viewed theater as a spiritual enemy rather than a Divine tool."

—ELIZABETH A. DAVIS
Actor and writer

"Bruce has articulated something in these pages that those of us in the professional theater world who identify as Christian have been trying to communicate for years. From the headwaters to the clouds, he has painted a clear and detailed picture of the theatrical ecosystem and the role people of faith can play in shaping global culture through the arts. Whether you are a Christian, agnostic, atheist, theater enthusiast, theater professional, or theater novice, this book is for you."

—JAKE SPECK
Executive director of A.D. Players at the George Theater

"Bruce Long's *The Problem with the Dot* succinctly and brilliantly outlines the structures upon which the American theater is built in a way that even someone who is completely unfamiliar with the theater business can understand. As an artist who works in the American theater, I also find the book creatively and spiritually inspiring. It reminds me of the sacredness of my calling and assures me that I am not alone in pursuing it."

—**CHRIS CRAGIN-DAY**
Playwright

The Problem with The Dot

The Problem with The Dot

A Holistic Approach to Christians' Care and
Cultivation of Global Culture through the
Theatrical Ecosystem

Bruce D. Long

Foreword by Makoto Fujimura
Preface by Wesley Vander Lugt
Afterword by Gillette Elvgren Jr.

WIPF & STOCK · Eugene, Oregon

THE PROBLEM WITH THE DOT
A Holistic Approach to Christians' Care and Cultivation of Global Culture through the Theatrical Ecosystem

Copyright © 2021 Bruce D. Long. All rights reserved. Except for brief quotations in critical publications or reviews, no part of this book may be reproduced in any manner without prior written permission from the publisher. Write: Permissions, Wipf and Stock Publishers, 199 W. 8th Ave., Suite 3, Eugene, OR 97401.

Wipf & Stock
An Imprint of Wipf and Stock Publishers
199 W. 8th Ave., Suite 3
Eugene, OR 97401

www.wipfandstock.com

PAPERBACK ISBN: 978-1-7252-8202-5
HARDCOVER ISBN: 978-1-7252-8203-2
EBOOK ISBN: 978-1-7252-8204-9

02/25/21

Scripture quotations marked NIV are taken from the Holy Bible, New International Version®, NIV®, copyright © 1973, 1978, 1984, 2011 by Biblica, Inc. Used by permission of Zondervan. All rights reserved worldwide.

Scripture quotations marked MSG are taken from *The Message*, copyright © 1993, 2002, 2018 by Eugene H. Peterson. Used by permission of NavPress. All rights reserved. Represented by Tyndale House Publishers, a Division of Tyndale House Ministries.

Scripture quotations marked NLT are taken from the Holy Bible, New Living Translation, copyright ©1996, 2004, 2015 by Tyndale House Foundation. Used by permission of Tyndale House Publishers, a Division of Tyndale House Ministries, Carol Stream, Illinois 60188. All rights reserved.

Scripture quotations marked ESV are taken from The Holy Bible, English Standard Version®, copyright © 2001 by Crossway, a publishing ministry of Good News Publishers. Used by permission. All rights reserved.

I'M GRATEFUL FOR THIS lineage of theatre artists who have heavily influenced my understanding of and deepened my passion for theatre: Dianne Murphree, Bruce Morgan, Gillette Elvgren Jr., Ralph Bryan, and Michael Rosenberg.

I'm indebted to these pastors and theologians who encouraged the notion of marrying my faith and art: Buddy Gray, Bill Price, Michael and Gail Simone, Jeremy Begbie, and Wes Vander Lugt.

One person, above all, conforms to the absolute truth of Holy Scripture and the highest ideals of the stage. I strive to be as authentic in faith and art as you, Michelle. I love you.

Contents

Acknowledgements | ix
List of Figures | xi
The Theatrical Ecosystem: An Overview | xiii
Foreword by Makoto Fujimura | xix
Preface: Theo-Theatrical Imagination by Wesley Vander Lugt | xxv

The Theatrical Ecosystem: An Introduction | 1
1. Headwaters: Theology and Theatre | 9
2. Lakes: Educational Theatre | 23
3. Oceans: Regional Theatre | 32
4. Clouds: Commercial Theatre | 48
The Theatrical Ecosystem: A Call to Action | 74

Afterword by Gillette Elvgren Jr. | 85
Bibliography | 87

Acknowledgements

THE EPIPHANY TOOK PLACE in New York City during the spring of 2015.

I was in town for the opening of *Doctor Zhivago*, the Broadway musical for which I was one of the producing partners. But the story actually started several months earlier.

During the fall of 2014, I had been in London promoting the musical *Memphis*, which we recently had opened in the West End. During my stay, Dr. Jeremy Begbie, a prolific author and scholar in the new field of theology and the arts, invited me to spend the day touring Cambridge with him. As a result of our day together, Dr. Begbie subsequently introduced me via email to Makoto Fujimura, an internationally renowned artist, writer, and speaker, who happened to have a studio in New York City.

Later, when we opened *Doctor Zhivago*, I accepted the invitation to join Mako and a few others for dinner at his studio. Mako's space was inauspicious and unpretentious yet alive with creativity—a working studio, to be certain, with paint and pigments and canvases in various states of creation. Though we had exchanged a number of emails, Mako and I had never met face to face, yet he welcomed me in with a table full of food and chopsticks. During our dinner conversation, he expanded on his thoughts of culture care, which is based on the premise that our culture is broken and needs care to be restored to retain wholeness. He made the correlation that caring for culture is akin to tending a garden. My eyes were opened, for all I had ever known was the

Acknowledgements

concept of culture war, a concept more synonymous with death than the generative work of caring for a garden. After dinner, I left with a signed copy of his book, *Culture Care: Reconnecting with Beauty for Our Common Life*, devouring it through the night more voraciously than I had the meal earlier that evening.

It is clear in this book that I am heavily influenced by, and borrow deeply from, Mako's teachings. The idea of a holistic approach to care and cultivation of global culture through the "theatrical ecosystem" is, in equal parts, an expansion of his teachings and a narrowing of the subject to focus exclusively on the art form of theatre. Much like Mako, I base my thinking and applications from a Christian perspective and often work with people within Christian communities. However, the theatrical ecosystem is not limited to Christians; the principles can be embraced universally.

I'm grateful for Mako's hospitality. He fed me much more than dinner that night; he fed my soul. Thank you, Mako, for the epiphany.

Finally, I would be remiss if I failed to acknowledge those who provided early editorial comment and research assistance: Gil Elvgren, Michelle Hoppe-Long, Meagan Hooper, Katherine Lee, Blake Long, Dave Reinhardt, Sharon Riggle, and Alexis Williams.

List of Figures

Illustrations

1. Water Ecosystem Illustration | 4
2. Theatrical Ecosystem Illustration | 5
3. Headwaters: Theology and Theatre | 9
4. The Dot Spectrum | 20
5. Lakes: Educational Theatre | 23
6. Student Graduating with Art Credit | 25
7. Schools Offering Theatre | 26
8. Theatre Graduates Annually | 28
9. Theatre Degrees | 30
10. Oceans: Regional Theatre | 32
11. Children's Theatre of Charlotte Front | 35
12. Children's Theatre of Charlotte Side | 35
13. The George Theater: A.D. Players Exterior | 36
14. The George Theater: A.D. Players Interior | 36
15. Lamb's Players Theatre Exterior | 37
16. Lamb's Players Theatre Interior | 37
17. Taproot Theatre Company Exterior | 38
18. Taproot Theatre Company Interior | 38
19. La Jolla Playhouse | 43
20. The McCarter Center | 44
21. Clouds: Commercial Theatre | 48

List of Figures

22. Broadway 2018–2019 Statistics | 53
23. West End 2018–2019 Statistics | 54
24. Theatrical Ecosystem Illustration | 74

Tables

1. Billion-Dollar Musicals | 57–59
2. Billion-Dollar Films | 61–64
3. Top-Grossing Christian Films | 65–66
4. Broadway Investment Results by Season | 69
5. S&P 500 Index Results by Year | 70
6. Theatre ROI | 71
7. S&P 500 ROI | 72

The Theatrical Ecosystem
An Overview

AN ECOSYSTEM, BY DEFINITION,[1] is a community of organisms functioning as a unit, one aspect of the community feeding into another in a cycle that is life-sustaining. By way of example: headwaters flow into lakes, which ultimately empty into oceans, whose waters evaporate to form clouds, providing regenerative rainfall along the entire ecosystem; thus completing the cycle. If even one component is unhealthy, then the entire ecosystem suffers.

This is true of the theatrical ecosystem, through which gardens of culture are cultivated at local, national, and international levels. Christians, specifically those of the Reformed or evangelical streams of Protestantism, have long neglected the theatrical ecosystem—a sin of omission perhaps, but nevertheless contributing to a degenerative global culture. This book expands the analogy of an ecosystem by unpacking the individual components of the theatrical ecosystem to:

- Help those with minimal exposure to theatre understand the indivisible construct of the theatrical ecosystem;
- Identify areas of neglect within each component; and
- Emphasize strategic corrections that will result in the holistic restoration of a healthy global culture.

1. *Merriam-Webster.com Dictionary*, "ecosystem," https://www.merriam-webster.com/dictionary/ecosystem.

The Theatrical Ecosystem

The health of an ecosystem starts at the source. If the source is corrupt, then everything that flows from it will be as well. Therefore, the headwaters are the source that influences every downstream component of the theatrical ecosystem. The primal source is Scripture, establishing the theatrical nature of the triune God throughout. Beyond the primal source are the relatively new headwaters of theology and theatre, in which both theologians and artists are strengthening the bond between faith and art. This is an important area of emphasis because these headwaters are populated with pastors, professors, authors, artists, and other thought leaders that shape the predominate Christian worldview towards theatre, and influence the level of Christian support for theatre artists and their work. Further, the erroneous segregation of art into secular or sacred has created a beaver dam that stymies the influence of regenerative artists. This prevalent obstruction needs to be dismantled.

The headwaters then flow into the lakes of educational theatre, with their relatively safe waters, where the next generation of artists coalesces for education and training within the theatrical ecosystem. Educational theatre begins in elementary school, continues through high school, and concludes with terminal degrees from conservatories and universities. However, private Christian schools, much like their public school counterparts, struggle to adequately support theatre programs and systemically deemphasize the variety of realistic career opportunities to students and families. Christian universities compound the preceding by offering limited degree options, resulting in a dearth of employable artists of faith. Strategic solutions include developing more rigorous and complete academic curricula with access to necessary theatrical facilities, and sourcing sufficient funding for endowments, scholarships, research, and portfolio projects. Without the purposeful development of qualified and properly credentialed arts leadership and theatre artists, the neglect of the theatrical ecosystem will continue unabated.

The lakes of educational theatre flow into oceans that are a confluence of all upstream waters. Within the theatrical ecosystem,

The Theatrical Ecosystem

new theatre graduates and seasoned professionals merge in the ocean of regional theatre. Regional theatres are hyper-local organizations that cultivate culture within their immediate communities. Regional theatre is composed of a variety of theatre types, from paid professional theatres to volunteer-driven community theatres. Regional theatre may be hyper-local in its scope and scale, but it is big business, contributing $2.6 billion to the US economy and reaching more than 44 million adults and children.[2] It is unconscionable to disregard this aspect of the theatrical ecosystem any longer.

In a healthy ecosystem there is an ever-changing distribution of clouds affecting the balance of the ecosystem. Commercial theatre is this distribution of clouds, which exerts influence by scattering regenerative rainfall in some places while forming powerful storms that reshape the theatrical landscape in others. Commercial theatre is a niche industry and global in scale with two major markets—Broadway in the United States and the West End in the United Kingdom—which have combined annual grosses of more than $4 billion and an audience of more than 65 million. However, global audiences exceed 600 million people, with cumulative grosses of more than $36 billion.[3], [4], [5], [6] The commercial theatre industry is often overshadowed by Hollywood's powerful public relations machine, which has led many financiers to mistakenly disregard theatre's better return on investment and generational culture care in favor of a "here today, gone tomorrow" Hollywood movie. But even Hollywood is actively adapting successful films into musicals in an effort to capitalize on the greener pastures of Broadway. This may be hard to believe, but was confirmed when Disney announced on the twentieth anniversary of *The Lion King* that the Broadway *musical*, not the animated *film*, has made more money than all the *Star Wars* films combined. By way of

2. Theater Communications Group, "Theater Facts 2017," 6.
3. Broadway League, "Statistics - Broadway in NYC."
4. Society of London Theater, "2019 Box Office Figures."
5. Broadway League, "Touring Broadway Facts."
6. Wax and Allan, "2018 Box Office Figures,"

comparison, *Star Wars* has grossed more than $9.5 billion globally, spanning ten feature films. According to Disney, "*The Lion King* has taken more money at the box office than any other stage show, or cinema release."[7]

Each chapter strengthens the case for a long-term holistic approach to the care and cultivation of global culture through the theatrical ecosystem. The final chapter of this book issues an immediate call to action for active engagement with two organizations that work in tandem for global regenerative culture care. Christians in Theatre Arts (CITA), a 501(c)(3) organization whose purpose is to "cultivate environments that empower and sustain all Christians in Theatre Arts,"[8] concerns itself with cultivating healthy theatre artists, empowering the next generation of theatre artists, and sustaining theatre artists who engage in regenerative culture making.[9] Meanwhile, The Repertoire Fund, a commercial theatre investment collective, is active in both the commercial and regional theatre spaces, solving two inherent challenges in commercial theatre investment: risk and speed to market. The Repertoire Fund: 1) minimizes the risk of one-off theatrical production financing by investing in a majority of the commercial theatre market over ten seasons, thereby realizing an above-average risk-adjusted return on investment, while cultivating regenerative global culture; and 2) increases speed to market for new commercial productions by establishing a national chain of regional theatres in order to:

- Control every aspect of the developmental pipeline;
- Control costs within the developmental pipeline via strategic partnerships with select educational theatres;
- Generate new revenue streams through monetized digital distribution of readings, workshops, and productions staged within the developmental pipeline; and

---

7. "Lion King Is Named."
8. CITA, "Purpose," https://cita.org/purpose.
9. CITA, "Theatrical Ecosystem," https://cita.org/theatrical-ecosystem.

The Theatrical Ecosystem

- Cultivate regenerative culture within local communities.[10]

The importance of this call to action is magnified by the unique opportunity currently presented by the 2020 global pandemic, which forced a hiatus on all theatrical productions worldwide. The market will reset, and artists will revive theatres. It is my prayer that when this grand reopening occurs around the globe, Christians are an integral part of the new beginning.

---

10. Repertoire Fund "Purpose," https://therepertoirefund.com.

Foreword

IN THE MID-1990S, SoHo in New York City was still the Mecca of the art world. On West Broadway—the main, glitzy patch of highly sought-after storefronts between Prince and Canal Streets—was Dillon Gallery, a relatively new gallery contesting in the Darwinian environment of commerce and art.

It was during this time that I moved into the city with my family, on Worth Street and West Broadway, as part of a church-planting effort by Redeemer Presbyterian Church. I was told, by many well-meaning Christians, to avoid going to New York City. To move my family there seemed as futile and unwise to them as turning back to Sodom and Gomorrah. But I followed the prophet Jeremiah's edict to "seek the peace and prosperity of the city to which I have carried you into exile" (Jer 29:7 NIV).

I distinctly remember praying that God would open the doors; later, when, at the appointed time, I knocked on one of the SoHo galleries interested in my work, with portfolio in hand, I found that the door was literally shut. The gallery closed their business soon after (a typical scenario for many new galleries).

So, when Valerie Dillon visited me in the studio after four years of knocking on literally closed doors, it was an answer to prayer. But a typical dilemma visited me, one that Bruce Long articulates well in this key work of understanding the ecosystem of the theatre world—*The Problem with The Dot*. How do we, as Christians, navigate the shark-infested waters of the art world of New York City?

Foreword

Valerie came into our studio below Canal Street in a summer dress, brought by a critic who wanted to show her the works of my studio mate, Hiroshi Senju. But Hiroshi kindly told Valerie to look at my works as well. I had just completed a Japanese screen piece on which I had blended verses of gold scripture into the landscape as if they were stars.

"What's written on here?" Valerie asked me, squinting to look at the words.

I took a deep breath. "It's Isaiah—a passage from the Bible."

She smiled and said, "I love Isaiah."

What people had warned me of, and what I had feared of the "pagan" art world rejecting God, turned out not to be true. Not entirely. Of course, people misunderstood Christianity and the cynical art world tended to reject it as a worn-out Western ideal. But what I experienced was God opening the door, and I walked right through it. And that door was opened by a non-Christian artist friend. Valerie exhibited my works in her gallery for more than a decade after that. And in that first exhibit in the heart of the art world, it was another critic, a self-proclaimed Jewish Buddhist, who wrote a glowing review in *Art in America*[1] that launched my career.

Certainly, there are battles, and surely, there is an invisible realm of spiritual battles. But culture wars waged by fears and anxieties to charge against the "enemy of culture," represented by the New York art world, turns out to be a false indictment. What Bruce describes as the backstage process of producing Broadway plays parallels what happens in the galleries and modern dance venues. If The Dot is too narrow, no production will neatly fit into the tight category of what "Christian" acceptability may be. Even if we want to "win" the culture for Christ, such "us-versus-them" mentality only makes prisoners of culture wars, if you can conscript artists to fight on the front lines. Our children will resist such a path, so even if we "win," we will lose the next generation. Culture wars will not create generative, enduring works of art. Such an effort will not create culture.

---

1. Kushner, "Hiroshi Senju and Makoto Fujimura."

Foreword

When I introduce myself to Christian audiences now, I say, "I am not a Christian artist." I shock people. For me, being a Christ-follower is the most important focus; I dare not use the word *Christian* as an adjective. It's time that the word *Christian* be the noun of our lives and culture.

The Dot, one might say, is an aggregate result of narrowing down the effect of the gospel to an adjective existence so we can market clearly to separate ourselves from the world, to create our own subculture. We project, as a result, an adjectival existence in the culture, such as in being a "Christian plumber" or even broadly to call ourselves a "Christian culture." God owns all the earth, the heavens, and the cultures. The Good Shepherd leads us *outside* our tribal safety (John 10) to the good nourishment of the cultural grass beyond the hills, where dangers do indeed dwell. That is why we, the sheep, need to listen well to the Good Shepherd and rely on his staff. This Dot problem, as Bruce accurately describes, involves both sides of the church-world debates. It's not just the dark realms of the art world, but it's also the theological problem of how we understand culture from a biblical base, and why we need to train our teenage sheep to create a new path for our tribe to enjoy. The paradigm must shift to change both sides.

This will require a change in metaphor. My proposal in *Culture Care* is to replace the culture wars language with metaphors of stewardship, care, and attentiveness. Such a metaphorical shift must be refined and injected into specific areas of the art world—such as theatre—so that culture care can be of pragmatic service to those who swim in those waters. Such a paradigm shift can help us to comprehend the theatre world as an important ecosystem to value and preserve for the churches at large and for a skeptical world that needs to hear the voice of the Good Shepherd.

Bruce honors my book *Culture Care* and the movement it has engendered, and he does the hard work of extending what I've written into the world of theatre. Bruce identifies the history and categories, of theatre, giving us a backstage tour of the inner workings and beautiful people that comprise these communities so that we can learn how to care for them. He is also a producer, and a producer's work is to make the effort as generative as possible financially and culturally. He encourages us to move beyond tribal boundaries into the margins of cultural realms where cultural nourishment is abundant. He is creating generative culture from within the system. He is leading us to pastures beyond our tribal limits, and he has the ear to hear the Good Shepherd's voice.

"Let imagination run wild," Bruce implores in response to Christians fleeing from culture of complexity, now trying to label even someone such as J. K. Rowling as one of their own, even though initially rejecting her as part of the forces of darkness because she uses witchcraft as a basis of her fantasy world. What Bruce is imploring is not to be undisciplined with our imaginations, but to be the opposite; unless Christians develop healthy imagination, they will simply allow it to be overtaken by commodifying forces or, worse yet, the spirit of darkness. A wise stewardship is first to name the thing in front of us, and then to let the imagination (or the biblical language for "heart") carry us to name and learn to love. Love can run wild only because love is at the heart of our relationship with God. God has created us to be creative, to have our loves run wild in the realm of the Spirit.

The Problem with The Dot is a reductionist problem: to force our understanding of culture from the perspective of a Christian conversion point, and to value the arts only as far as useful for discipleship and evangelism. A typical Christian statement is, "Let's reclaim the culture," as if it were a sinking ship. But culture is not separate from us, even if we sequester and shield ourselves from its "evil." Culture *is* us. We are on the same sinking boat.

In our churches and parachurches, for example, we now have a plethora of discipleship programs for becoming a "Spirit-filled Christian." While we work hard as individuals to attain the fruits of the Spirit (Gal 5:22), we never ask how our culture is doing. Even if we speak of the culture within the church, such a pointed question can be revealing. How are we doing in the culture of the church, especially as seen by the world and our children? Instead of love, we are seen as people of hate. Instead of peace, we want to demonize the other. Instead of patience, we want quick fixes. Instead of kindness,

Foreword

we have been divisive. Instead of faithfulness, we have unfaithfulness and abuses in our leaders. Instead of goodness, we have injected fear into culture. Instead of self-control, we have become known for our angry outbursts of self-righteousness. I am not against individual programs for spiritual growth, but we have largely failed to grow the fruit of the Spirit into the world. Culture is us. By developing a cultural "estuary" of diversity and by valuing competition and complexity, the church can be part of the Spirit's work to birth culture from which the future generation can benefit.

We have assumed an individualistic stance on defining our success to "combat culture." We are, as a result of such individualistic efforts, but scattered dots in culture without any connected tissues. We assume, just because we call ourselves "Christians," that the fruit will somehow manifest itself in our culture and affect the larger cultures. Theatre, to be good, must capture all of humanity, not just what is allowed in Sunday school skits. The Bible is full of drama, mystery, and intrigue. There are, certainly, boundaries of ethics, and there is a difference between depicting evil and participating in evil. But such a fluid definition of a "successful cultural endeavor" needs a broader and more comprehensive allowance (or the Spirit's patience) to operate. We shall ultimately be known by our fruits. If the fruit is good—and even if the production is all by atheists—a Christian can partake gladly with thanksgiving to the Father, who pours his gifts into all people.

The word for shepherd in Greek is *poimen*—(Good *Poimen*)—a lovely sister word for *poiema*, which I translate as "poetry or masterpieces." So, when Saint Paul addressed the Ephesian church by writing, "For we are his workmanship, created in Christ Jesus for good works" (Eph 2:10, ESV), I translate the first half as, "You are God's masterpieces." The Good Shepherd already has made us as beautiful, resonant poems to speak into the anxious, cynical world. God's theatre is to bring such prismatic communal light, refracted by each of us, into the heart of darkness, and this book is a map for such extra-tribal journeys.

Makoto Fujimura

Preface

Theo-Theatrical Imagination

WHAT DO THEOLOGY AND theatre have in common? For much of church history, the common answer was "very little" or, stated more pessimistically, "the ever-present danger of idolatry and duplicity." A few voices demurred, affirming the inherent theatricality of theology and the inherent theological quality of theatre, but it wasn't until the 1980s that sustained and profitable dialogue emerged between these two disciplines.[1]

Several decades later, this dialogue has cleared away debris that had been preventing the biblical and theological headwaters from flowing into and sustaining a healthy theatrical ecosystem. Bruce Long has wisely shown that when each part of this ecosystem is healthy, there is a beautiful symbiosis between theology and theatre that moves us beyond The Dot of mere "Christian theatre" toward a robust vision and practice of global culture care.

Given the long history of animosity between theology and theatre, however, it seems fitting to say a few more words about how they inform and complement each other in order to set the stage for Bruce's important work, beginning with some definitional clarifications.

---

1. On the theatrical side, a prominent example is Victor Turner's *From Ritual to Theater: The Human Seriousness of Play* (1982). On the theological side, the watershed moment was the publication of Hans Urs von Balthasar's *The Theo-Drama: Theological Dramatic Theory* (1988–98).

Preface

Theology, on the one hand, is not merely an intellectual exercise. Christian theology in particular is reflection on action as we seek to embody the way of Jesus. The goal of theology is to build beautiful character and improvise faithful action within the cosmic divine drama. We do not engage in theology apart from the rough-and-tumble realities of real life; we do so as characters embedded within the developing theodrama. In short, *theology is faith seeking performative understanding*.[2] As such, it is inherently theatrical.[3]

Theatre, on the other hand, is not merely a rote exercise of memorizing lines and delivering them before an audience. Theatre seeks to express invisible realities within the earthiness and immediacy of real, visible interactions.[4] Theatre is a process of bringing everything a person is (including faith commitments) into everything the story and characters require. Building a character for stage overlaps with the dailyness of putting on Christ in real life.[5] Good acting requires receptivity to unseen forces, spiritual dynamics, and the sacredness of personal encounter. You might even say that *theatre is performance seeking theological understanding*.

If theology is faith seeking performative understanding, then theatre is a gift to show theologians (and everyone is a theologian!) what it looks like to embody a story and develop it in company with others. For those seeking to build godly character, theatre models the kind of discipline, intentionality, and receptivity required to move from who I am in the flesh to who I am in this new creation story. Theatre is a gift to show the church—or any community, for that matter—the power of embodied presence, proximity, and interaction to transform us emotionally, intellectually, socially, and spiritually.

---

2. This riffs on a definition often attributed to Anselm: "Theology is faith seeking understanding."

3. For a brief introduction to why theology is inherently theatrical, see Vander Lugt and Hart, eds., *Theatrical Theology*, xiii–xiv.

4. Peter Brook calls this the "holy" and "rough" aspects of a "living theater." Brook, *Empty Space*, 15.

5. Rom 13:14; cf. Col 3:12.

Preface

If theatre is performance seeking theological understanding, then theology is a gift to show theatre artists how every story is a participation in the universal Story of creation, de-creation, and new creation. Just as all human dramas, aware or unaware, participate in the universal theodrama and its cosmic conflict, so all theatrical productions, aware or unaware, participate in the universal production of the Spirit and the battle with powers and principalities. Theology guides theatre artists in staying attuned to the spiritual significance of human encounter and communion, conflict and resolution. At the same time, theology keeps those in theatre receptive to the ongoing dangers of idolatry, duplicity, and deadly repetition.

To locate theology and theatre within the same ecosystem, as Bruce does in this book, reveals the need for a robust theo-theatrical imagination. Rather than keeping theology and theatre in separate conceptual and performative worlds, a theo-theatrical imagination embraces both the inherent theatricality of theology and the inherent theological quality of theatre; it moves us beyond The Dot to embrace every moment and space, whether on stage or off stage, as a possibility for divine encounter.

The Problem with The Dot advances this theo-theatrical imagination and provides compelling rationale for Christians to embrace theatre in its fullness at every level and in every form. Equipped with theo-theatrical imagination, theatre artists, patrons, theologians, and Christian leaders can be freed to receive all theatre as a gift to advance God's mission of restoration and renewal. It's time to demolish The Dot and cultivate theo-theatrical imagination for the life of culture and the glory of God.

Wesley Vander Lugt

The Theatrical Ecosystem

An Introduction

HANDS ON A HARDBODY was my first Broadway production as a producing partner. It is a beautiful Broadway musical with a salacious title that received three Tony Award nominations. The ensemble cast of characters features an eclectic mix of humanity, including an evangelical Christian who prays and worships, and is overtaken by the Holy Spirit, which manifests in uncontrollable laughter. She is even able to reach the story's bigoted, drunken, and downright mean antagonist, who experiences forgiveness and salvation in the end. This unintentionally evangelical musical was impeccably written by Pulitzer Prize– and Tony Award–winner Doug Wright, Trey Anastasio, and Amanda Green. The authors take great care that every character is authentic without even a hint of caricature or prejudice.

After every Broadway opening, the producers convene the "morning after" meeting, which includes the various marketing companies and public relations firms. It can be celebratory or somber depending on the opening night. Our "morning after" mood was somber, frustrated, and angry. Around the table were some of the best minds and most financially successful Broadway producers working in the industry today, and, while we all agreed *Hands on a Hardbody* is a good musical, we sat dumbfounded. The box office was dismal, and the mixed reviews were not going to provide the juice a Broadway musical needs to boost sales and get through

The Problem with The Dot

the Tony Award season. The problem before us was clear: How do we save this show? We floated suggestions. We argued ideas. We discussed and discarded plans. Nothing seemed right. I know I'm supposed to ask a question, but I'm nervous. I've heard my entire life how much showbiz and Christianity are at odds. The conversation around the table continues and I can't muster the courage to participate. Yet, I know my question must be asked. Silently, I raised my hand and the beehive of the room came to a full stop. Every head turned to me.

"Why haven't we engaged the Christian community? Our protagonist is an evangelical Christian and our antagonist experiences a conversion. This is exactly what we want to see." There, I said it, and even included myself—"*We* want to see."

The room held for a beat. I watched as a realization spread across the faces in the room. Reaching out to Christians had never once crossed anyone's mind and the novel idea was suddenly viable. Given the green light, I initiated a faith-based campaign to save the show. I booked church groups, performances on national and international television, and engaged writers for Bible study curriculum. Unfortunately, it was too little too late, and the show closed prematurely—but not before garnering a few Tony Award nominations.

Moral of the story: I was afraid to say something because I believed the false narrative that the theatre industry is antagonistic towards the faith. We lost a show in part because the producing team failed to consider a Christian audience. I will never forget the realization racing around the room that morning, because it, in turn, sealed my own realization: The theatre industry isn't *antagonistic* towards Christianity; it's *agnostic* towards Christianity.

I believe the residue of dispensational theology and the prevailing literalism of the evangelical community are, in large part, responsible for this agnosticism. Before exploring contemporary theatrical and religious agnosticism, perhaps a brief overview of the intersection of theatre and church history will be helpful. As early as 970 CE and throughout the Middle Ages, religious drama flourished in medieval theatre. Shortly after the Middle Ages, the secularization of England began when Henry VIII broke from the

The Theatrical Ecosystem

Roman Catholic Church and established the Church of England with himself as the head. Anglicanism was part of the Protestant Reformation that was cutting away at the influence of Roman Catholicism and culminated with Elizabeth I, a staunch supporter of theatre, ending the Catholic claim to the English throne. The monarchy increasingly tightened its legal control over theatre during both Queen Elizabeth's and King James's reigns, to the point where only members of the royal family could sponsor theatre. A civil war between the monarchy, Charles I, and the Puritan-backed parliament ended the English Renaissance in 1642 when the Puritans—who vehemently opposed theatre, denouncing it as a den of immorality—outlawed all theatrical activity. King Charles was beheaded and the nobility was exiled. Though the theatre returned during the Restoration, its denouncement remained intact.

This disenfranchisement continues to manifest in contemporary society in pseudoscriptural phrases such as "in the world, but not of the world," a phrase that I remember hearing so clearly in my youth. This mantra justified the neglect of a culturally generative art form. More inclusive application of Scripture should have served warning that withdrawal is neglect, and the results are a culture that is degenerate, suffocating, and in need of oxygen. Perhaps more devastating than the neglect is the creation of a "Christian art" subculture that siphons attention away from global culture care. This artificial dichotomy has only served to marginalize Christian artists and minimize their voices in the global conversation. The conundrum for many artists of faith then is to create ever-narrowing stories in which the antagonist is just bad enough to create minimal conflict while the protagonist abdicates to *deus ex machina* resolutions. Christian audiences have been conditioned to accept Scripture-brought-to-life stories or poorly told contemporary parables in which salvation solves it all, each rarely escaping the mediocre Christian entertainment niche. This further insulates the audience and forces creatives into perpetuating evangelistic messaging that has less and less regenerative effect on global culture. We must reverse course, recognize a neglected

The Problem with The Dot

culture, and tend to it through the power of "a good story well told"[1] that reengages individual hearts of the global community.

This calls for Christians to invest themselves in culture care through art in general, but more specifically via theatre. Theatre, as such, is not exclusive to Broadway, or the Broadway tour at a city's performing arts center, or even the local high school musical. Rather, theatre is a complete system of indivisible academic, technical, and creative disciplines dependent upon each other to function, much like a water ecosystem.

An ecosystem, by definition, is a community of organisms functioning as a unit, one aspect of the community feeding into another in a cycle that is life-sustaining. Consider the following simplified environmental ecosystem as an example: (1) headwaters flow into (2) lakes that ultimately empty into (3) oceans, which evaporate to form (4) clouds that provide rainfall necessary to regenerate the entire ecosystem. These four components compose an ecosystem that, when clean and healthy, provide life and quality of life in the form of oxygen and beauty, respectively.

Illustration by Maggie B. French

1. McKee, *Story*, 21.

The Theatrical Ecosystem

Extensive use of the ecosystem analogy will provide insight and understanding with regards to the full scope of theatre as a global cultural art form by defining the components of the theatrical ecosystem, identifying areas of Christian neglect within the theatrical ecosystem, and detailing the strategy for implementing a holistic approach for the care and cultivation of global culture through the theatrical ecosystem.

Illustration by Maggie B. French

1. Headwaters: Theology and Theatre

The sources of the theatrical ecosystem are the "headwaters," composed of theologians and artists tasked with renewing and strengthening the intellectual, theological, and artistic relationship between faith and theatre arts. In addition, the headwaters influence the formation of future artistic, academic, and theological leadership born from downstream.

2. Lakes: Educational Theatre

The headwaters directly influence the downstream lakes of educational theatre, where the next generation of artists coalesces in relatively safe and calm waters as they mature in their art. Educational theatre consists of the full spectrum of training for the next generation of artists—beginning as early as introducing the art form in elementary school, through credentialed mastery of the art form with a terminal postgraduate degree. Culture care of the lakes is the purposeful formation of the next generation of artists.

3. Oceans: Regional Theatre

Once these playwrights, directors, designers, performers, and other creatives have graduated from conservatories, universities, and seminaries, they have a choice to make. A small yet influential number will head upstream and populate the headwaters as the next generation of theological and academic leadership. However, most will continue downstream, emptying into the vast oceans of regional theatre, where the majority of artists live and work, cultivating the culture of their local communities in the process. Specifically, the senior leadership of regional theatres, the artistic director, should be an area of intense focus as this position is the single most influential cultural voice at the local level.

4. Clouds: Commercial Theatre

Ultimately distilled from the ocean of regional theatres around the world, commercial theatre completes the cycle of the theatrical ecosystem by drawing new works from regional theatre and transferring them to a commercial stage. These clouds float high above the balance of the ecosystem, moving at will around the planet, providing nourishing rainfall and occasionally developing into significant storms with the capacity to reshape the theatrical landscape. New plays and musicals opening on Broadway, London's West End, domestic and international tours, or even off-Broadway

The Theatrical Ecosystem

(commercial theatre) are first developed at the local level before transferring to the international commercial market. The new play or musical, when produced on the commercial stage, regenerates the entire theatrical ecosystem by academicians who cite the work in their research as well as educational and regional theatre productions for local communities. Further, the revenue from each commercial theatre production is distributed to investors and royalty participants, including back to the regional theatres responsible for the initial development. Commercial theatre also replenishes the theatrical ecosystem through the commissioning and acquisition of new plays and musicals, whose creation is traditionally funded, in part, by commercial producers using both educational and regional theatre throughout the developmental process.

This book examines how the theatrical ecosystem influences and cultivates local and global gardens of culture as well as how Christians are broadly negligent in stewardship of this ecosystem. Unquestionably, this neglect has resulted in an ecosystem bereft of the beauty and balance found in Christian beliefs. This neglect is in opposition to the original mandate of humanity set forth in the creation account found in the opening chapters of Genesis, specifically: "The Lord God placed man in the Garden of Eden to tend and watch over it" (Gen 2:15, NLT). The wisdom of this scriptural poetry is that dual interpretations apply simultaneously. Because the Garden of Eden was then the whole of existence, it is reasonable to extend the Garden of Eden to include all of planet Earth as the whole of contemporary existence. When this scripture is taken literally, humanity has a mandate to care for the intricate and various environmental ecosystems that nourish physical life on our planet, ensuring a healthy life for those living now and for future generations. Equally important is the interpretation in which humanity has a mandate to care for the intricate and various artistic ecosystems that nourish the culture of our planet, providing the soul of humanity with an oxygen-rich aesthetic that makes our physical life worth living. Beauty, then, is oxygen. Therefore, artists and entrepreneurs, creatives and financiers, clergy and laity must act in equal measure to cultivate a healthy theatrical ecosystem that supplies beauty to local and global gardens of culture. Tangentially, one should also consider that "God created human beings in his own image" (Gen 1:27, NLT). Since God is an image maker, our creative mandate is to make images and metaphors that include all language, all written words, and all works of art. Our essential prerogative, then, is to tend to this image-making process to glorify him. This is an act of formative creation that regenerates the culture and garden in which we live.

In the following sections, the theatrical ecosystem will be unpacked to understand the necessity of each component within the whole and to emphasize specific areas of neglect for the purpose of identifying strategic corrections that will restore the delicate balance required to sustain the health of global culture. A full embrace of the theatrical ecosystem will be manifested in the strategic deployment of artistic, financial, and scholarly resources across the entirety of the theatrical ecosystem, thereby ensuring the longevity of the art form and perpetuating financial rewards while cultivating a healthy global culture.

1

Headwaters

Theology and Theatre

Illustration by Maggie B. French

THE SOURCE OF THE theatrical ecosystem is the headwaters composed of theologians and artists tasked with identifying and strengthening the intellectual, theological, and artistic relationship between faith and theatre arts. Additionally, these thought leaders shape the formation of future artistic and academic leadership. Foundational to embracing the headwaters is understanding the past and present relationship of theologians and artists, how this relationship shapes a predominant worldview within Christianity regarding the arts, and how it influences Christian education and church leadership.

Theologians and Artists

Headwaters are the small, uppermost source for creeks, streams, and rivers, which flow through lakes and eventually empty into oceans. Headwaters are essential to every other component of the ecosystem. As with all life, Christians recognize Scripture as foundational. It is important to identify the primal source for the headwaters of the theatrical ecosystem within the sacred text. In *Performing the Sacred*, Dale Savidge surveys theology and theatre roots in Scripture.[1] One of the earliest examples is Psalm 118, which is essentially a script complete with dialogue, stage direction, and given circumstances of a biblical performance written around 1044 CE. Other examples include David's performance as a wild man in 1 Samuel 21; Joab's turn as both playwright and director in 2 Samuel 14; a prophet in full costume, coupled with method acting in 1 Kings 20; the meeting of Elisha and the king of Israel in 2 Kings 13, which foreshadows the physical theatre training found in the Suzuki method; and—perhaps the most overt recording—in Ezekiel 4, where God uses the prophet to stage a full production complete with set, props, costumes, blocking, and dialogue. Insofar as the gospel narrative is concerned, it may be worth noting that while Jesus does not specifically mention theatre, he does employ the art form when he performs the role of a traveler on the road to Emmaus in Luke 24. Recognizing these select scriptural references, God's written revelation demonstrates a theatrical dimension. This theatrical dimension of God is the primal headwaters.

---

1. Johnson and Savidge, *Performing the Sacred*, 25–30.

Headwaters

As a natural ecosystem has multiple headwaters that ultimately consolidate into creeks and rivers before finally emptying into oceans, so too does the theatrical ecosystem have multiple sources that flow through the balance of the ecosystem. Today these headwaters may be divided into several sources that, when considered as a whole, are often referenced as "theology and the arts." Several prominent theologians and artists have established, and are currently strengthening, the connection between theology and the arts.

To understand the context in which theatre sits comfortably within the theological realm, it is useful to reference foundational works outlining links between theology and the arts that more generally precede the emerging work of theology and theatre.

Francis Schaeffer, an American evangelical Christian theologian and Presbyterian pastor, establishes a contemporary foundation in the 1973 publication of *Art and the Bible* when he writes, "The lordship of Christ should include an interest in the arts. A Christian should use the arts to the glory of God, not just as tracts, mind you, but things of beauty to the praise of God."[2] Schaeffer expands this relationship through extensive research by documenting the correlations to art (visual, music, film, and literature) and culture from the Roman Age through the present in his bestselling book and influential accompanying film, *How Should We Then Live?: The Rise and Decline of Western Thought and Culture*. It is this work that initially identifies the division in our society resulting in a broken culture and attempts to identify the causes. Within less liturgical churches, Schaeffer is often credited as the first to give theology permission to engage with culture.

Schaeffer's contemporary and friend Hans R. Rookmaaker released his illuminating classic, *Modern Art and the Death of Culture*, in which he contemplates ambiguity about art among Christians and ambiguity about faith among artists, while also discussing the role Christian artists can play in proclaiming truth through their work. However, it was Rookmaaker's 1978 work, *Art Needs No Justification*, published posthumously, that provided

---

2. Schaeffer, *Art and the Bible*, 18.

The Problem with The Dot

context for understanding art's place in society and what it means to be a Christian artist in the world.

The 1980s introduced two important works: Calvin Seerveld's *Rainbows for the Fallen World* (1980) and Frank Schaeffer's (son of Francis Schaeffer) *Addicted to Mediocrity* (1981). Seerveld is emphatic that a deep abiding relationship with God is just as important as skill and talent. Moreover, Seerveld makes the point that artists' works need not contain any specific or overt Christian message. Schaeffer issues a stinging rebuke that Christians have sacrificed the artistic prominence they once enjoyed for centuries and have settled instead for mediocrity.

The turn of the century introduced theologians and artists actively caring for theology and the arts today, beginning with Jeremy Begbie's collection of essays, *Sounding the Depths: Theology Through the Arts* (2002), in which theologians and artists argue that part of theology's responsibility is to engage with culture, but particularly the arts. David Taylor also brings together a varied group of theologians and artists who discuss the kinship between the church and the arts, and how to foster that relationship, in a pragmatic collection of essays, *For the Beauty of the Church* (2010). In 2017, Taylor realigns John Calvin's thoughts to build a theological foundation for liturgical arts in the church in *The Theater of God's Glory: Calvin, Creation, and the Liturgical Arts* (2017). Meanwhile, Begbie adds to his vita by releasing *Redeeming Transcendence in the Arts* (2018), which focuses generally on the transcendent nature of the arts and how Christian involvement in the arts can be shaped by God's transcendence through Jesus Christ.

Arguably, the most influential work to date is *Culture Care: Reconnecting with Beauty for Our Common Life* (2014), by internationally renowned artist, author, and speaker Makoto Fujimura. Two sentences from Fujimura's book sum up the foundation on which much of this book is built: "Culture is not a territory to be won or lost but a resource we are called to steward with care. Culture is a garden to be cultivated."[3] This book is intended to build upon Fujimura's thoughts and extend his metaphor beyond that of a singular

---

3. Fujimura, *Culture Care*, 22.

garden in need of tending into a more holistic approach of cultivating global culture by caring for the entire theatrical ecosystem.

Theology and the arts is a general theme of study inclusive of visual arts, music, film, literature, and theatre. A seminal book, *The Liberated Imagination: Thinking Christianly About the Arts* (2005), by Leland Ryken brings together a meaningful and even inspirational approach to the full spectrum of the arts in general. Theology and theatre can be seen as a unique stream of the more general headwater, but even theology and theatre contains multiple unique sources: (a) the Catholic stream; (b) the Orthodox stream; and (c) the Protestant stream, which may be further divided into two specific streams—the liberal Protestant stream and the evangelical/Reformed stream. The Catholic and Orthodox streams generally have been stronger in developing theology of the visual arts following an aesthetic of the eye often resulting in contemplation, while the Protestant stream has been stronger in developing theology of literary arts that follows an aesthetic of the ear that results in obedience, as exemplified in this scripture:

> Do not merely listen to the word, and so deceive yourselves. Do what it says. Anyone who listens to the word but does not do what it says is like someone who looks at his face in a mirror and, after looking at himself, goes away and immediately forgets what he looks like. But whoever looks intently into the perfect law that gives freedom, and continues in it—not forgetting what they have heard, but doing it—they will be blessed in what they do. (Jas 1:22–25, NIV)

William Dyrness, in *Poetic Theology* (2010), recognizes that all human beings hunger for beauty or possess an aesthetic sense. The Catholic and Orthodox aesthetic provides a vision of the drama while the Protestant aesthetic allows for participation in the drama. However, theatre is a mimetic art form that must be both seen and heard in order to experience its fullness. Theatre requires both contemplation and participation. It is this aesthetic tandem that has instigated a leeriness of theatre built upon dual dangers of idolatry (visual) and immorality (participation) onstage. The danger of this duality is compounded by the performance's influence of the audience, resulting in a general disenfranchisement between Protestant evangelical/Reformed Christians and theatre. Therefore, the balance of this book is referencing the Protestant evangelical/Reformed stream when addressing Christians' neglect of and reengagement within the theatrical ecosystem.

Theatre as a formally recognized art form has existed since ancient Greek society and is present in every single contemporary culture. Yet Christian involvement has been sporadic through the centuries, intensifying with the church's use of theatre in the Middle Ages; a movement of sorts of poetic drama by Christian playwrights in the 1940s and 1950s, with Christopher Fry, T. S. Eliot, Dorothy Sayers; and most currently the Willow Creek Community Church drama movement of the 1980s through early 2000s.[4] However, the origins of theology and theatre as headwaters are, by comparison to the art form, in their infancy; these new springs really began bubbling up in late 1970s and early 1980s. The importance of these headwaters and their influence over water quality and flow downstream, coupled with Christians' wholesale neglect upon this source of the theatrical ecosystem, cannot be overstated. It is essential to establish a foundational bibliography of theologians and artists who helped establish these headwaters, continuing through those who care for them today.

From 1988 to 1998, the American edition of Hans Urs von Balthasar's five-volume *Theo-Drama: Theological Dramatic Theory* was released. In this comprehensive work, Balthasar, a Swiss theologian and Catholic priest, works through the history of dramaturgy to frame the drama of salvation, God's incarnation, and the relationship between God and the individual with the help of theatrical categories. Balthasar is credited with beginning the formal subject of theology and theatre through his work by determining that if God's revelation and salvation are interactive words and actions on the world stage, then theatre should be used to understand God's action in the world. Almost as a footnote, Max Harris's *Theater and Incarnation* (1990) offers a meditation of the theatricality

---

4. Sherbondy, "What Happened to Drama," paras. 1–2.

of the incarnation, arguing that both biblical and dramatic texts should be approached with the same theatrical imagination.

By the late 1990s and early 2000s, the headwaters of theology and theatre were truly taking shape. Prolific playwright Gillette Elvgren Jr. contributed a series of essays that broached the subjects of: (a) "Can I Hear a Witness? Docu-Drama: A Model for Christian Theater" (1998); (b) "The State of the Arts: A Symposium" (1999); (c) "Theatrical Conventions: Rediscovering Transcendence in Theatre " (2004); and (d) "How Then Shall We Write?" (2004). In Chicago, the Willow Creek Community Church drama movement was well underway, in which Willow Creek Church spearheaded the use of the theatrical sketch as a sermon teaser, and published several notable books for churches and schools of their fast-moving and often comical sketches produced within the last 25 years. Elvgren and Willow Creek Community Church collaborated on a full-scale musical, *Jairus*, which opened at the church in April 2000, selling more than 40,000 tickets[5]—a unique moment in contemporary church history.

Sam Wells, in his thoughtful and thought-provoking book, *Improvisation: The Drama of Christian Ethics* (2002), establishes theatrical improvisation as a model for Christian ethics that extends beyond the individual to encompass the church. Kevin Vanhoozer further explores theatrical elements in relationship to theology in *The Drama of Doctrine* (2005). Vanhoozer seeks to restore the Bible and doctrine as dual sources of authority for the church via the metaphor of drama, articulating that the role and benefit of doctrine is the holistic integration of the Christian to himself or herself, to others, and to God.

One of the more accessible reads is *Performing the Sacred: Theology and Theatre in Dialogue* (2009), by Todd Johnson and Dale Savidge. The authors explore the intersection of spirituality and theatre by providing a historical overview of the relationship between Christianity and theatre, identifying theological themes that are present in theatre (incarnation, community, presence), explaining why alternate forms of media will never usurp live

5. Pareti, "Willow Creek Show Strong," line 2.

theatre, and exploring common suspicions between actors and churches that have resulted in mutual alienation.

The year 2014 was a prolific and important year for the headwaters. Shannon Craigo-Snell's *The Empty Church* (2014) brought together theatre directors and theologians in a work that extends church beyond the sanctuary and into life by emphasizing that liturgy encourages Christians to step into various roles and enables intellectual and willful choices regarding those roles in society. Expanding on the foundation of Balthasar's *Theo-Drama*, Wesley Vander Lugt provides an excellent summary of recent developments in theology and theatre in his similarly titled thesis, *Living Theodrama: Reimagining Theological Ethics* (2014), and in a collection of essays coedited with Trevor Hart in *Theatrical Theology: Explorations in Performing the Faith* (2014). Of particular note in *Theatrical Theology* is Todd Johnson's essay, "Doing God's Story: Theatre, Christian Initiation and Being Human Together," in which he draws a correlation between the work of the actor and that of Christians who choose to "put their lives into the ongoing story of God's redemption and play the role of Christian disciple,"[6] knowing that the story is of value to the audience.

Kevin Vanhoozer follows up his 2005 publication, *The Drama of Doctrine*, with *Faith Speaking Understanding: Performing the Drama of Doctrine* (2014), in which he contends that "the ultimate aim of theology is to form not simply competent (i.e., knowledgeable) but also excellent (i.e., wise) actors in the drama of redemption. The wise disciple is the one who discerns and enacts in new, contextually appropriate ways the same truth, goodness, and beauty that is God's reconciling love in Jesus Christ."[7]

The last sentence of Vanhoozer's quote forms a cornerstone of this book. Christians who wish to be "wise disciples" will discern the theatrical ecosystem is suffering from neglect and will realize their involvement is a "new and contextually appropriate way" to restore the system with the same "truth, goodness and beauty"; thus creating a dynamic church-theatre relationship that cultivates

6. Johnson, "Doing God's Story," 89.
7. Vanhoozer, *Faith Speaking Understanding*, 205.

regenerative global culture. This book implores Christians to invest artistically, financially, and academically in cultivating the theatrical ecosystem as mandated in Scripture (Gen 2:15) and supported at the primal source of the ecosystem.

Theologians and Artists as Thought Leaders and Definers of Worldview

It is worrisome to see bestselling authors peddling self-help books ostensibly as "Christian inspiration" to the masses. It is time to provide substantive thought and art for the soul. It is time to provide beauty to a culture suffocating in thick pollution; beauty is oxygen.

Many of the theologians and artists mentioned in the preceding section may be writing for a more academic and comparatively smaller audience. However, more concentrated efforts must take place to find "translators" that can communicate their message beyond the halls of academia to get in touch with the masses. Theologians and artists are engaging the prophetic responsibility of reshaping the caricatured worldview of evangelicals. Contrary to this view, but in accordance with Fujimura's writings, Christianity should not be engaged in a culture war. Culture, like a healthy garden, is cultivated with great care. No culture can survive a destructive force like war; there are no beneficiaries. Those who understand the transcendent nature of the arts realize that where the heart leads, the head is quick to follow. By contrast, Christians' overwhelmingly singular pursuit of political power as a means of legislating culture is incomplete because laws are an external force that produce compliance of the head with the heart slow to follow. Dietrich Bonhoeffer, in *The Cost of Discipleship*, spends a great deal of time addressing the notion that obedience cannot be divorced of faith or vice versa; the two are intrinsically linked. Christians need to embrace the idea that political influence and culture care are married. If laws are intended to produce mindful obedience in forming a more perfect union, then theatre is intended to inspire humanity's spirit in establishing and maintaining such a utopia. It is time to level the scales with as much strategic involvement and financing as fundamentalism's political ambitions have received since the early 1930s. Religion and the arts share a common spirituality in that both strive to illuminate and inspire. Therefore, the Christian's focus on the theatrical ecosystem for the purpose of cultivating life and quality of life for our global culture is as important as political aspirations, and more authentic to being made in the image of our Creator. Live theatre, especially when infused with the Holy Spirit and Scripture, speaks to the heart with the power to inspire individual change from the inside out. Live theatre reminds us what it means to be human and in community. Live theatre reflects and reveals, in equal measure, our relationship to others, and often to God.

Christians must prayerfully and steadfastly resist the predominate idea that being "in the world but not of it" necessitates stark divisions that they must ultimately win for the "cause of Christ." Remember, culture is not a war to be won or lost. Rather, Christians should toil to instill a new paradigm in which the formation of the mind (through obedience to legislation) and the desires of the heart (inspired through the arts, but specifically theatre) are aligned for the deeper and more complete understanding that to be Christian—that is, to be like Christ—is to bring life and quality of life to this long divided world. Beauty resides in the unity of Christ, which bridges the great divides among us. Beauty is oxygen. Oxygen begets life. Beauty begets quality of life.

Creating life and quality of life for the global culture through the care and cultivation of the entire theatrical ecosystem is the work of theology and theatre; it is the work of story theologians. When theologians and theatre artists are working in tandem, this is Christian leadership to change the world.

Influencers of Christian Education Leadership and Church Leadership

The single worst victory that Satan can have is to convince Christians that artists honor God only when creating music, books, films, and theatre exclusively for Christian audiences. Theologians

Headwaters

and artists must help Christian education and church leadership recognize and reject the long con that has led conventional wisdom to believe in a distinct separation between sacred and secular art. As one born in a newly desegregated Alabama, I recognize "separate but equal." Yet, Christians exalt this punishing policy like it is a trophy:

- She's a brilliant author; she's the "Christian" J. K. Rowling.
- Her music is so good; she's the "Christian" Adele.
- What a movie! He's the Spielberg of Christian film.

So-called Christian art is a toxic doctrine in which Christian art is sanctioned from the pulpit so Christian consumers never have to sully their hearts, minds, or souls with what "secular" artists produce and vice versa.

It is imperative that Christian education leadership and church leadership reject such distinctions, for God alone is sacred and it is he who first created without such distinctions. Indeed, God is an artist who crafted all of humanity in his image. Humans house a deep, innate desire to be like their Creator, longing to create that which is beautiful and eternal. Christians should do so with abandon. Let imaginations run wild. Create masterpieces that transcend preconceived notions of "Christian" art. God promises in Proverbs 22:29 (ESV):

> Do you see a man skilled in his work? He will stand before kings; He will not stand before obscure men.

Theologians and artists must help Christian education leadership and church leadership understand that by encouraging, creating, promoting, and endorsing only Christian music or Christian films—or even Christian theatre—from the pulpit and through Christian school curriculum, they perpetuate the downward spiral into the mediocrity Frank Schaeffer assailed. They also simultaneously relegate artists to a micro-niche of subgenres that mutes the Christian voice in the broadest global cultural conversations. Christian artists must refuse to be marginalized in order to appeal exclusively to a smaller subset. Artists and theologians cannot

The Problem with The Dot

stand by and allow art to be divided into "sacred" and "secular." The former is confined narrowly to "The Dot," explained below, while the latter encompasses everything else.

Imagine a spectrum that moves from darkness to light, left to right. At the far left is the label "Atheist." At the far right is another, "Fully devoted disciple of Christ." In the center of the spectrum is an extremely tiny mark—The Dot—that, when magnified, is the singular spot where there is statistically more light than darkness on the spectrum. The Dot represents the exact moment of salvation for the evangelical Christian. Sharing the gospel is such a prominent aspect of Christian culture that The Dot receives an inordinate amount of attention—so much so that The Dot becomes the whole of existence for Christian audiences and financiers. Art that is created for the sole purpose of evangelism is sanctioned as sacred art. Anything else is secular art and cannot be sanctioned formally by the church. It is unfit for Christian artists, audiences, patrons, and investors.

The problem with The Dot is that there is no room within its borders for anything other than overt conversion to Christianity. In reality, any time someone moves from darkness towards light, the Great Commission is in action. This is made clear in Acts 26:17–18 (MSG):

> "I'm sending you off to open the eyes of the outsiders so they can see the difference between dark and light, and choose light, see the difference between Satan and God, and choose God. I'm sending you off to present my offer of sins forgiven, and a place in the family, inviting them into the company of those who begin real living by believing in me."

Headwaters

When the atheist becomes an agnostic, the heavens rejoice. When the agnostic moves into doubt, the heavens rejoice. When the doubter believes, the heavens rejoice. When the believer's faith is strengthened, the heavens rejoice. Anytime anyone slides to the right, the heavens rejoice. All art that moves a person from darkness to light is the sacred work of the Holy—not just art created within the confines of The Dot.

Theologians working in tandem with artists must prayerfully yet relentlessly remind Christian education leadership and church leadership that they are shepherding and preparing artists, whose work God values as much as any ministry or vocation. These regenerative artists have the God-ordained prophetic voice, authority, and responsibility to lead the reconciliation and healing of our global communities by cultivating life and quality of life. This is art—and while not "sacred," it is formative, and thus beneficial to the edification of Christ and his body of believers.

Clearly, the church and Christian education cannot condone evil, injustice, and depravity—all of which should be considered deformative art. But artists of faith must intimately understand the human condition so that they may appropriately and effectively speak the truth through their art. Christian artists can offer freedom to those in shackles, but only if these artists are close enough to apply a soothing salve when those tight chains release their cold grip. This is the tightrope artists of faith walk when emulating the image of the Creator.

In practical application, Christian education must be about preparing the next generation of artists with the qualifications necessary to acquire gainful employment in the global theatre industry. Meanwhile, churches must anoint, and perhaps even ordain, theatre artists for regenerative work in educational theatre, regional theatre, or commercial theatre without expectation that these artists will return to "full-time Christian ministry" or, worse, create propaganda for the sake of The Dot. Further, the church should encourage prayerful financial support of and commissions for their artists that are equitable to that given for any missionary, parachurch organization, or faith-based non-profit. Imagine the transformational results

The Problem with The Dot

if churches supported an artist-in-residence rather than sending a young member off to seminary. Consider how transformational it would be to global culture if seminary curriculum required training in arts appreciation and artistic outreach methodologies for the local church and Christian schools.

Until the above can be realized, non-profit organizations such as CITA (Christians in Theatre Arts) must bridge the gap.[8]

---

8. See this book's final section, "The Theatrical Ecosystem: A Call to Action," for details on how CITA is working within the theatrical ecosystem for the formation of Christian theater artists.

2

Lakes

Educational Theatre

Illustration by Maggie B. French

THE HEADWATERS OF THEOLOGY and theatre directly influence the downstream lakes of educational theatre, the second component of the theatrical ecosystem. Educational theatre consists of the full spectrum of training for the next generation of artists, beginning as early as elementary school and concluding with the Master of Fine Arts (MFA) and other terminal degrees from conservatories, universities, and seminaries. Not only must the next generation of artists master the art form, but they must also adopt a regenerative mandate as artists of faith.

Role of Secondary Educational Theatre

High school, middle school, and even elementary school are the first points of contact many students have when it comes to theatrical arts exposure and training. This is the time that introductory learning happens, and love of theatre is instilled. It is through robust curriculum and performance opportunities at school that students are able to first foray into theatre arts. Not all will decide to train at the collegiate level, but participation at the secondary level—whether on stage, behind the scenes, or as an audience member—can create a lifelong appreciation for theatre and cultivate the next generation of theatergoers, theatre supporters and donors, and even future board members.

Beyond traditional training in the basics of the craft in theatre classes or afterschool enrichment, elementary and secondary school drama programs additionally foster *life skills through theatre skills* for the greater student population. Stepping into a theatre experience allows students a time to practice social interaction. In each class, they immerse themselves in a world where listening is key; awareness of others is always necessary; and social cues in body language, tone, and inflection are discussed and dissected. The children who have the opportunity to be a part of theatrical training become independent critical thinkers and problem-solvers as they gain confidence and self-esteem. They learn empathy, examine motivations for choices and actions, and discuss the consequences in a safe and guided environment, while also becoming strong public speakers. Theatre, therefore, becomes more than a craft; it becomes a way to grow good people who care for others and the world around them. It helps them to understand the importance of seeing those who may not be seen and caring enough to take action.

Lakes

The perspective through which this training is done, then, becomes key. Theatre shapes thinkers. Theatre presents life on stage, and good theatre has conflict. There is good and bad, light and dark; yet somehow, while the Bible is full of stories that can be challenging in this way, Christian schools cannot stomach a modern story with similar themes but will tolerate paper-thin biblical depictions on the stage. Theatre is an art form that asks hard questions, provokes reactions, and starts difficult conversations. Because of this, theatre can be a difficult art form or educational program to manage in Christian schools, which are typically private, tuition-based institutions, and espouse a responsibility for protecting the minds and hearts of the children in their care. Safeguards are put in place for young people. Everything from language to story line is scrutinized and sanitized to make sure it is not offensive to the viewer or the performer.

In this, we do a great disservice to what theatre was created to do, and the wonderful learning opportunity for this key area of the theatrical ecosystem. This is a chance to search for a redemptive work that may be messy and conflict ridden, but allows truth to be told on stage, and not just in a Bible story format. This is the age at which the seeds of the ecosystem are planted, tilled, and fertilized with care to encourage growth and make deep roots.

To truly shore up this area of the theatrical ecosystem, Christian schools need to have an understanding not only of the art form, but also of the powerful tool it can be in helping children grow into responsible adults. There needs to be an awareness of just how powerful theatre can be in the development of community and culture.

One of the key responsibilities of schools that want to support and develop a theatre program is knowing how to hire qualified teachers who can create a scope and sequence that builds theatrical training in acting as well as the technical arts. The curriculum should be brave enough to endure conflict and tough conversations in order to bring quality scripts to their students and school communities.

If Christians are to train the next generation of artists, we must educate Christian schools and parents about what theatre training entails and the process by which one reaches the top of his or her game in the theatrical disciplines. The overall infrastructure—and understanding of how to create the adequate scope and sequence of programming, how to hire qualified teachers, how to create a school's theatrical culture and support system—can be as critical to student success as the training itself. Further, schools and parents should emphasize that actors make up only a small fraction of the theatre industry. Educators must encourage future directors, stage managers, lighting designers, sound designers, costume designers, scenic designers, and even producers, in order to help students create a healthy view of the immense collaboration it takes to create theatre, but also to realize the incredible number of jobs the industry sustains.

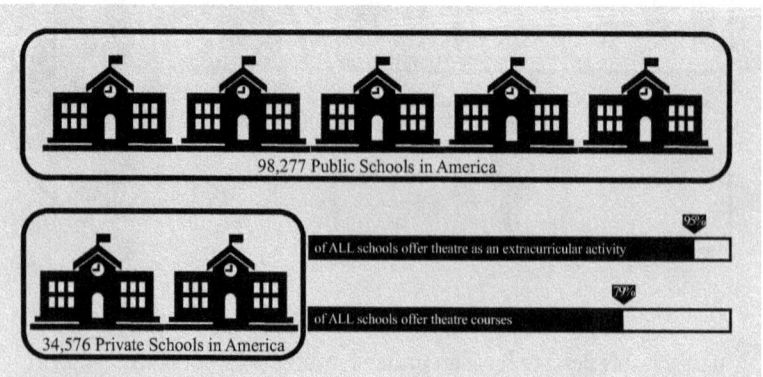

Throughout the country, middle and high school theatre programs have opportunities to compete at one-act play festivals and individual event competitions. These are wonderful places for students to receive outside feedback, interact with other theatre students and programs, and gauge their training against that of their peers, particularly the ones that may be pursuing theatre at the next level, or ones they may see in the college audition circuit. Much like sports, it provides college resume-building and, also, scholarship opportunities. By way of example, Christians in Theatre Arts (CITA) holds an annual secondary theatre festival with students from across the country. In conjunction with Christian colleges, CITA was able to offer students in acting and technical arts more than $225,000 in scholarships. However, the opportunities for students from Christ-centered schools to participate are precipitated upon the assumption that school administration and parents have a culture-care mindset about participation—that, from an early age, students, families, and schools see the theatre industry as a mission field. As others may go into what we consider the traditional mission field and assimilate with indigenous groups, so must our students learn at an early age to be well trained in their craft to gain the respect of those around them.

Role of Undergraduate Programs and Degrees

As secondary theatre students feed into higher education, the first question they must consider is whether to pursue a Bachelor of Arts (BA) or a Bachelor of Fine Arts (BFA). The difference is between a generalist degree that teaches all aspects of theatre, allowing students additionally to major and minor in other areas (BA), or a conservatory approach, where a student must audition or interview to get into one of the highly coveted spots to train in a specific discipline (BFA). The majority of Christian colleges and universities have BA programs in which students can train broadly in a liberal arts setting. This broad-based learning is key for creating well-rounded students that have a greater knowledge of the world around them and an understanding of how that knowledge informs their art. Majors are not only performance based, but also include theatre education and technical theatre, or even theatre criticism and dramaturgy.

Few Christian colleges and universities have coveted BFA programs, mainly because of the expense and expertise needed for accreditation. A BFA in musical theatre performance, for instance, may be required to have dance, music, and acting professors teaching everything from ballet and tap to jazz and social dance, music theory to private voice, and history of musical theatre to advanced acting in particular methodologies. Within a BFA, or a conservatory training program, a small cohort is chosen—typically 20 or less—with preprofessional training in mind. The idea is that graduates will work in the industry upon graduation. As programs develop more connections and graduate more students who become working professionals, these programs become increasingly more prestigious, desirable, and selective with those auditioning. Thousands may audition across the country for one BFA program, and the cost and percentage of college rejections can pile up for prospective students and families.

Within the theatrical ecosystem, access is an issue, particularly when so many are training at such a high level in conservatory programs across the country in non-Christian institutions. There are only a handful of faith-based BFA training programs in the country, and, training aside, with the emotionally vulnerable nature of the art form, programs without a biblical foundation can be catastrophic to the student artist when it comes to self-esteem and value in an industry filled with rejection. Students in BFA programs are competing at a higher level, vying for summer stock work at professional theatres to build their resumes, and jockeying for roles in conservatory, college, and university productions. Training, work ethic, and recommendations can mean the difference between a robust resume and someone scrambling to work on a show. This part of the theatrical ecosystem is when artists are created, and students determine whether or not they are really cut out to work in the industry. When looking at many of the top lists of theatre programs—while one or two in the rankings may have a Christian or faith-based affiliation—none of the most prestigious theatre programs currently ranked are those grounded in teaching and training with a Christ-centered worldview, and none are from an evangelical program. If the top talent in the United States is clamoring to get into the best schools, how can some of these Christian college programs compete? How do they even get on the radar?

If the cost of private school education at the secondary level were not enough of a hurdle, students fortunate enough to be selected for some of the most prestigious programs (New York University, Carnegie Mellon University, and Yale University) can find themselves right in the middle of the student loan crisis this country is experiencing. After four years studying theatre and stepping into a contract-to-contract–based industry, it can be a difficult reality for students who wish to pursue a calling in theatre that they simply cannot afford to do so. Access to opportunities is built for the "haves" much more than the "have-nots." Christians must look at this area of the theatrical ecosystem as an opportunity to support the next generation of artists through the establishment of scholarships and proper infrastructure so that those who have the talent and desire are able to train in their theatrical calling and mission field.

Role of Graduate Programs and Degrees

While many may move into professional opportunities after college graduation, others will move into higher learning for additional training. Graduate school is a place that offers a deep dive into the

The Problem with The Dot

theatrical discipline of choice, and students can opt for either a two-year (typically) Master of Arts or a three-year (typically) Master of Fine Arts (MFA). The MFA is the arts equivalent of a PhD and sets the student up to teach at other colleges and universities in their discipline, in addition to opening access for more academic areas of study like theatre history and dramaturgy (the theory and practice of dramatic composition). Students can delve into graduate-level work in playwriting, acting, Shakespeare, musical theatre, or any specific area of technical arts (lighting design, sound design, costume design, scenic design) or an area such as theatre administration. All disciplines prepare the students to work professionally in the industry, or, in the case of theatre administration, run a theatre company or even produce theatre commercially.

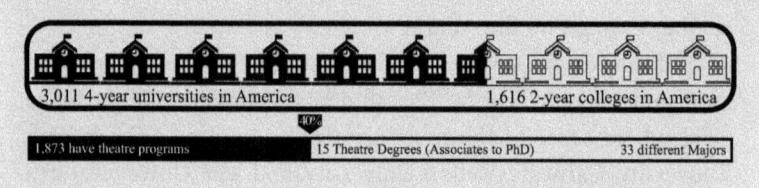

Graduate school not only provides further training, but also plays a key role in the theatrical ecosystem for those that will step back into education as instructors. However, professional experience is coveted in college and university instructors. Again, connections with the industry are key. MFA programs are popping up at Christian institutions of higher learning, such as at Regent University, where graduates have established themselves in the industry and provided key contacts for students as they look for internships. Such schools provide a showcase opportunity for artists with industry agents and directors. At the same time, when economic conditions change, it always seems to be the arts curriculums that are cut first, and degreed graduate programs are reduced to drama clubs and minor-emphasis offerings. This lack of prioritization, even in the face of financial considerations, reinforces Christian's agnosticism of theatre as an important global culture-making artform.

Lakes

As narrow as the opportunities are at the undergraduate level, the road at the graduate-school level becomes even narrower. How can we perpetuate the health of the theatrical ecosystem and ensure that—from elementary and secondary education through graduate school—students have access not only to opportunities, but also to scholarships and funds to afford those opportunities? How can we accomplish those goals while also establishing programs that can compete with the best of the best? Conservatories, universities, and colleges are the single most important sources of formation for the next generation of artists. They are where they will establish their worldview, which, by extension, influences their art at the next level. As with the headwaters of theology and theatre, Christians have, in large part, neglected the academic component of the theatrical ecosystem, thereby abdicating a seat at the table. While many Christian universities have theatre departments, not a single Christian or faith-based theatre conservatory in the world can compete with the Julliard School, Yale School of Drama, or any other theatre conservatory of merit. Christians have little influence when it comes to training the next generation of artists and arts leadership, and—while some working in the industry graduated from theatre programs in faith-based universities—the limited numbers entering the workforce and the lack of networking between them is crippling the potential influence of their work.

3

Oceans

Regional Theatre

Illustration by Maggie B. French

THE TERM "REGIONAL THEATRE" encompasses a myriad of different types of theatres, but the key element linking all regional theatres is their non-profit status as recognized by the Internal Revenue Service. All regional theatres are hyperlocal, with significant influence over the culture of their immediate community.

Types of Regional Theatre

The League of Resident Theatres (LORT)[1] is the largest professional non-profit theatre association, with 75 member theatres located in every major market in the United States, including 29 states and the District of Columbia. Member regional theatre companies allow LORT to administer the collective bargaining agreements with various unions, including the Actors' Equity Association (AEA or "Equity") for actors and stage managers, the Stage Directors and Choreographers Society (SDC) for directors and choreographers, and the International Alliance of Theatrical Stage Employees (IATSE) for scenic, costume, lighting, sound, and projection designers and technical artists.

However, hundreds of non-profit professional theatres that are not members of LORT populate cities and communities throughout the country. The important distinguishing factor between professional non-equity (or non-union) theatres is how actors, directors, designers, and other creatives receive compensation for their work. One will find flourishing community theatres throughout the United States as well, but—while the work may be good quality—community theatres do not pay actors and typically do not have budgets that can support professional design and construction in all areas. Community theatre's primary task is the preservation of the art form by staging the classic musicals and plays with and for the community. Lay actors and creatives find a home on the community theatre stage as do audiences who yearn to see their family members, friends, and colleagues in productions.

The regional theatre movement, established in the mid-twentieth century, was born out of a desire to expand beyond New York City's commercial theatre market to create smaller theatre companies that could produce more artistic and socially conscious work without the pressures of commercial viability. Today, non-profit regional theatres bring theatre to the masses by connecting to the people within local communities. Regional theatres understand the power of the art form to cultivate culture for their communities,

1. For more, see http://lort.org.

The Problem with The Dot

and they also value the role they play in developing the personality of their communities. Thus, regional theatres will have mission statements for their companies that distinguish the type of work they do. This specificity in mission helps to guide programming for a theatre season, and ultimately determines the actors, directors, choreographers, stage managers, and designers they will need for the work. Many theatres will address needs they see within their community and the organization may even double down on their own values as community values shift. We have seen keen examples of this throughout the United States as theatre companies have put stakes in the ground regarding political and social issues that have flooded the headlines in an effort to further values they hold dear and shift the culture within their city. Whether it is ensuring representation on stage through a commitment to equity, inclusion, and diversity, or promoting female playwrights and directors in the midst of the #MeToo movement, regional theatre is a force at the local level that can shift culture and values within that community.

Other theatres may focus on subject areas like new works or stories from a specific point of view. One burgeoning regional theatre field is theatre for young audiences (TYA). Professional regional theatres are producing and performing work written and directed for children and families. Typically serving children younger than 18 and their families, TYA companies put work on their stages that connects with specific ages. This may include baby theatre, which is sensory rich and interactive, for newborns to toddlers; theatre for the very young, which introduces preschool and early elementary grades to theatrical storytelling; and even teen-specific theatre, which has more mature themes and complicated plots. Prevalent in most TYA companies is a connection to literature adaptation of popular titles that children read at home or in school. Because of this, and the smaller cannon of TYA work, new work development is a key component at many of these companies. Particularly the larger and more influential companies in the United States, such as Children's Theatre of Charlotte[2]—a company dedicated to new work development—make sure the storytelling

---

2. For more, see https://ctcharlotte.org.

Oceans

on its stages are works told from the child's point of view, or that children have great agency in the story and decision-making in the play. This can empower young people experiencing theatre. While past TYA fare has been fairytale retellings, current work for young audiences has become sophisticated, with European and Australian theatres leading the way. This newly developing component of the theatrical ecosystem should be an area of strategic attention for significant culture care and cultivation.

Courtesy of Charlotte-Mecklenburg Library

The Problem with The Dot

A smaller subset of regional theatre is the Christian or faith-based theatre company. While many small—often one-person—companies have popped up sporadically in recent years, there are really three faith-based theatre companies of merit currently operating in the United States and one in Canada:

A.D. Players at the George Theater (Houston, TX)

Photographs by John Gabriel

Founded in 1967, A.D. Players is the oldest and current flagship Christian theatre company in the United States, with a full season of seven productions and educational initiatives running year-round in the new $18 million George Theater, which includes an advanced rigging system, cutting-edge lighting, state-of-the-art sound systems, and a spacious lobby and concession area.[3]

Lamb's Players Theatre (Coronado, CA)

Photographs by Nate Peirson and copyright by LPT

Founded in 1971, Lamb's Players spent the early years as street theatre until 1986, when it ended 15 years of touring street theatre. In 1994, Lamb's Players Theatre opened as the resident theatre

3. For more, see https://www.adplayers.org.

company in the beachside community of Coronado. It currently offers a five-show season.[4]

Taproot Theatre Company (Seattle, WA)

Photos by Boone Speed Photography (boonespeed.com)

Founded in 1976, Taproot began as a touring group and has developed into Seattle's largest midsize theatre company. It

---

4. For more, see https://www.lambsplayers.org.

currently offers a five-show season, touring programs, and educational initiatives.[5]

Pacific Theatre (Vancouver, BC)

Founded in 1984, Pacific Theatre offers an eight-production season and a mentorship program, but no other educational initiatives.[6]

Based on the limited number of theatres and locations, establishing more faith-based theatre companies is a logical area of expansion for Christians. However, all these companies started 50–60 years ago and function today as traditional regional theatres. That is to say, their current programming is not exclusively Christian content. Current economics would not support the growth of a theatre market that exclusively produces overt evangelical or Christian programming, and an underfunded theatre company's limited cultural influence would not net a return on the investment. Regional theatre programming must appeal to the local community-at-large to sustain a viable business model. Considering the general disenfranchisement of most Christians to theatre, faith-based theatre companies quite simply appeal to such a narrow segment of the local community (The Dot) as to be unsustainable. Rather, I'm advocating that, much like the legacy theatre companies previously listed, new theatre companies expand the scope of programming and cast a wider net in the regional theatre scene rather than establishing more "Christian" companies. We should establish transformational regional theatre companies that offer a variety of plays and musicals, work for Christian artists, and alternatives to the raw and offensive (deformative) fare of traditional regional repertory theatres. Such companies would set the stage for playwrights who cannot find venues for more conservative story themes.[7]

5. For more, see https://taproottheatre.org.
6. For more, see http://pacifictheatre.org.
7. See this book's final section, "The Theatrical Ecosystem: A Call to Action," for a plan of how this will be practically implemented.

The Problem with The Dot

Role of Regional Theatre in the Local Community

The goal of regional theatres is threefold. Within each goal lies the focus by which each regional theatre will not only produce its work on the stage, but also connect with its local community.

Engage the Community

Regional theatres work to reflect the pulse of the community and the diversity reflected in it through their choice of stories they bring to the stage. It becomes a critical point of the work of the theatre to find ways to connect with its community and partner with other cultural and community organizations to be a relevant player in the city's growth and maturity. It also becomes critical from a funding perspective at the local, state, and national levels as funders are looking for both quantitative and qualitative data to support reasons to contribute to the non-profit work the theatre is doing. Whether it is coproducing a work that tours into secondary schools about generational alcohol and drug abuse, or partnering with the professional ballet to bring a new work to the stage that reflects the history of the Latino community, funders want to see how regional theatres engage the cities in which they are planted and why they are valuable to their communities to be convinced that they are worthy of foundation money.

Educate the Community

Regional theatres educate the community by providing arts access and arts education opportunities. Educational connections can happen in many ways, from student matinees with reduced ticket prices and talkbacks or workshops after the show, to in-school residencies and full education academies within the theatre to train school-aged youth or adults in acting and technical theatre. As the professional theatre entity within the community, the regional theatre's educational programming is an additional way to (a) promote community engagement, (b) get to know the city and the people in it, (c) connect more deeply with patrons, and (d) to continue building audiences with younger families, thereby inspiring the next generation of artists. One important element is the additional revenue that educational initiatives and programming provide, often at a much higher return on investment than ticket sales. Educational programming then becomes a revenue stream for non-profit theatres to bolster their budget, while giving back to the community.

Entertain the Community

Regional theatres entertain the community by providing an opportunity to bring diverse people together for a shared, live theatrical experience. The communal experience is unique to theatre because each performance is live and the audience different every night, so together the experience is new every time. Knowing their community and creating the balance between what their audiences want and what they think their audiences should see is the difficulty in creating the theatrical season. Theatre seasons traditionally include one or two tentpole[8] productions that are popular titles to carry the season so that other shows on the calendar can be new, experimental, avant-garde, artistically challenging, or socially important shows. While entertaining the community is important, it is really about cultivating the culture of the community and, in the process, earning the trust and loyalty of their patronage. Creating this culture, while arduous and time consuming, results in fewer tentpole productions and a healthy symbiotic relationship in the conversation between the stage and the audience. La Jolla Playhouse in California has done this extremely well, creating a cultural appetite for new works in development and an expectation that those new works will transfer to commercial success on Broadway. This appetite for new works educates patrons as to their responsibilities in the developmental process, including active audience support (i.e., sold-out performances) of first-look

---

8. See *Merriam-Webster.com Dictionary*, s.v. "tentpole."

productions and providing feedback throughout different iterations of the same show. Such audience collaboration prepares the show to transfer to Broadway and potentially win a Tony Award.[9] There is pride in the shared experience and buying a ticket becomes more than entertainment—it provides life, and quality of life, to the local community.

As mentioned, regional theatres such as La Jolla Playhouse or some of the larger TYA companies may undertake the arduous task of new work development. This is how new plays and musicals are added to the cannon of theatrical work. The developmental process can take anywhere from two to ten years. Many new works will live in the regional theatre realm and go on to be picked up by theatrical publishing companies, which then will license those shows for other regional theatres, universities, and even secondary schools to perform, while other works will transfer to a commercial production on Broadway, off Broadway, or in London's West End.[10]

Relationship of Regional Theatre to Educational Theatre

A regional theatre in formal relationship with a university, while somewhat rare, is not unprecedented. The advantages of partnerships between professional theatres and universities include shared venues that host professional productions and student performances, and interdisciplinary collaboration in the form of:

- Theatre professionals who teach or serve as guest lecturers in the classroom
- Faculty members who participate as expert panelists, scholars, and strategic partners for the regional theatre's productions and educational activities

---

9. Exemplified by La Jolla Playhouse's success with *Jersey Boys*, *Memphis*, and *Come From Away*.

10. See chapter 4 for more information about the development of new work for the commercial stage.

Oceans

- Student internships to assist in rehearsals, shop work, administration, or other educational programs
- Creative exchanges among theatre industry professionals, academic departments, students, and faculty

Notable regional theatre companies that are housed on university campuses include:

1. La Jolla Playhouse[11] in partnership with the University of California at San Diego

Courtesy of La Jolla Playhouse

- Tony Award for Best Direction of a Musical, *Come From Away* (2017)
- Tony Award for Best New Musical, *Memphis* (2010)
- Tony Award for Best New Musical, *Jersey Boys* (2006)
- Tony Award for Special Theatrical Event, *Billy Crystal's 700 Sundays* (2005)
- Tony Award for Best New Play, *I Am My Own Wife* (2004)

11. See https://lajollaplayhouse.org/.

The Problem with The Dot

- Pulitzer Prize, *I Am My Own Wife* (2004)
- Tony Award for Best New Musical, *Thoroughly Modern Millie* (2002)
- Regional Theatre Tony Award (1993)
- Tony Award for Best New Musical, *Big River* (1985)

2. The McCarter Center[12] in partnership with Princeton University

Courtesy of Thomas Miller

- Tony Award for Best New Play, *Vanya and Sonia and Masha and Spike* (2013)
- Pulitzer Prize (1937, 1938)
- Regional Theatre Tony Award (1994)

---

12. See https://www.mccarter.org/.

3. Yale Repertory Theatre[13] in partnership with Yale University
   - Tony Award for Best Direction of a Play, *Indecent* (2017)
   - Tony Award for Best New Play, *Fences* (1987)
   - Pulitzer Prize (1987, 1990)
   - Regional Theatre Tony Award (1991)

While there are limited partnerships such as Abilene Shakespeare Festival in June on the campus of Abilene Christian University,[14] research did not reveal a single Christian university formally partnered with a year-round professional regional theatre company. This must change as the benefits are extensive. The esteemed reputation, financial upside, internship opportunities, and long-term employment success of students far exceed the challenges of shared space and resources. This area of collaboration within the theatrical ecosystem can be cultivated by creating new partnerships with established Christian universities or by establishing a faith-based conservatory that is competitive with the most renowned theatrical conservatories in the world. These partnerships would be considered fully developed when the programming includes a year-round LORT theatre company, student cabarets and productions, off-campus productions, educational initiatives for the local community, special events, and Broadway/off-Broadway touring.

To accommodate the programming of a fully developed partnership, the facilities should be given significant consideration and budgetary support for construction and maintenance. A standalone theater is insufficient without the appropriate auxiliary space supporting the venue. The campus of a regional theatre company in partnership with a university, such as those regional theatres recognized above, typically includes:

---

13. See https://yalerep.org/.
14. See Abilene Christian University, "Abilene Shakespeare Festival."

- A minimum of two venues[15]:
    1. Mainstage (506 seats on average)
    2. Blackbox (up to 300 seats depending on configuration)
- Dressing rooms for stars and ensemble
- Scenic shop with direct access to loading docks and venues, including:
    1. Carpenter's area
    2. Welder's area
    3. Painter's area
    4. Costume shop
    5. Prop shop
    6. Lighting/sound shop and storage
- Administrative offices
- Rehearsal studios
- Lobby with merchandise and concessions areas
- Restaurant/bar/courtyard
- Off-site climate-controlled storage for costumes, props, scenery, etc.

Cultural and Economic Impact of Regional Theatre

An estimated 1,855 professional non-profit theatre companies in the United States contribute more than $2.7 billion to the US economy and attract an audience of more than 39 million adults and children annually.[16] Nationally, the cultural and economic impact of regional theatre is outstanding. However, the regional theatre is a hyperlocal product specifically designed to engage, educate,

---

15. Some have presenting theaters with a minimum of 1,100 seats, but typically with 2,000–2,500 seats.

16. Voss et al., *Theatre Facts 2018*, 1–6.

and entertain the immediate community in which it resides. The economic impact study "Staging Cleveland: A Theater Industry Study" demonstrates the cultural influence and economic impact 12 theatre companies had on the city of Cleveland and Cuyahoga County, Ohio:

> The overall economic impact of the Cleveland Theater sector in 2015 includes a total of 2,382 direct employees and an associated $58.9 million in labor income, as well as $471.7 million in output impact. From this direct impact, the Theater sector accounted for 5,065 total jobs. 1,815 indirect jobs represent the supply chain and are comprised of industries that sell their products and services to the Theater sector. 868 jobs identified in the induced effect reflect employment in Cuyahoga County due to household purchases of those employed in the Theater sector and its supply chain. The total labor income of the Theater sector was $234.8 million. The total value-added impact of the Theater sector was $377.9 million. The total output impact was $903.2 million. In terms of taxes, the Theater sector was responsible for $67.9 million in 2015. Of the total $67.9 million, $23.6 million was in state and local taxes, and $44.3 million was in federal taxes. Data from the market research firm SDRS revealed that roughly 580,000 individuals that lived in the Cleveland Designated Market Area attended a live Theater event in 2015. This equates to 37 out of 100 households viewing live Theater that year.[17]

---

17. Lendel et al., "Staging Cleveland," xiii.

4

Clouds

Commercial Theatre

Illustration by Maggie B. French

IN A HEALTHY ECOSYSTEM, an ever-changing distribution of clouds influences the Earth's energy, balance, climate, and weather by regulating temperature and spreading the sun's energy evenly across the Earth's surface. In addition to adding beauty to the skies, clouds can carry the perfect snowfall for a picturesque Christmas, or form into storms with the power to alter landscapes. This is true of the theatrical ecosystem as well. Commercial theatre moves above, scattering beauty yet also influencing and reshaping the cultural landscape.

As in an environmental ecosystem, the lifecycle of a new Broadway musical begins and ends in the earlier components of the theatrical ecosystem. It is helpful to understand the stages of the commercial theatre lifecycle and how it impacts the entire theatrical ecosystem before, during, and after premiering on the commercial stage. It should be noted that every show is unique in how it journeys toward global commercial exploitation, but the following is a good representative sample of the process.

Discovery

A producer may discover a new work through relationships with playwrights and composers, a private reading, a university or regional theatre workshop, or even an independently produced performance at a theatre festival.

Development

Once the producer has optioned the piece, he or she moves it into development. How far along the piece is at the time of discovery will be a major factor in determining how long development will take. The most rudimentary form of development is a reading. This is so common that the Actors Equity Association has created the "AEA 29 Hour Reading" contract in which actors have a maximum of 29 hours to rehearse and perform the new work. The reading cannot use any costuming, blocking, or memorization. The next level of development will be a workshop in which some memorization, rough blocking, indicative costuming, and a few musicians may be added. These two levels can be repeated or interchanged as often as necessary. To control costs, these are often produced in partnership with universities or regional theatres.

The Problem with The Dot

Out-of-Town Tryout

Theatre is a collaborative art form that is not limited to the creative staff and cast. Eventually the new piece needs an audience. The out-of-town tryout is a commercial performance anywhere outside New York City. This was the norm during the 1940–1960s, when out-of-town tryouts were produced in Philadelphia, Boston, Princeton, and other cities in the tristate region surrounding Broadway. However, that all changed in the 1970s when producers found it more cost efficient to partner with non-profit regional theatres. A few prominent regional theatres have since shaped—and now control—the path to the commercial stage. La Jolla Playhouse (La Jolla, California) is considered by many to be the flagship regional theatre in the United States, but others include 5th Avenue Theatre (Seattle), Steppenwolf Theatre (Chicago), Arena Stage (Washington, DC), The A.R.T. (Boston), and Alliance Theatre (Atlanta). Keep in mind that La Jolla Playhouse is located on the campus of the University of California, San Diego and The A.R.T. is on the campus of Harvard University. This is not an entirely uncommon precedent and one that will gain ground as educational theatre and regional theatre continue to take advantages of successful partnerships.[1]

Commercial producers line up to stage new works with regional theatre companies prior to Broadway for a number of reasons, including:

1. The quality of productions
2. The caliber of the technical crew and facilities
3. The regional theatre's LORT designation for controlling labor costs
4. The company's cultivation of audiences that understand how to contribute to the process of preparing a new work

Producers provide an enhancement, or financial contribution, typically in the range of $500,000 to $2 million to the regional

---

[1]. See the "Relationship of Regional Theater to Educational Theater" section in chapter 3.

Clouds

theatre's production budget to give the regional theatre a Broadway cast and creative staff they could not otherwise afford. The result is an enhanced production staged as close to the full-scale commercial production as possible in an affordable and safe environment far from early critical reviews. The enhanced production is produced without the possibility of return on investment in exchange for a qualified test-market run of the new commercial production. If all goes well, the enhanced production will transfer to the commercial stage with the costs of the enhanced production absorbed as a line item in the full capitalization of the commercial production. If, through the out-of-town tryout, the producer determines the show is not commercially viable, then the producer will either find an alternate path to commercial viability or abandon the project altogether. As with any research and development, the prevailing wisdom is that it is better to spend a little on the enhancement and try to get it right than to lose the full capitalization on the commercial stage if it's not ready. In recent years, multiple regional theatres have pooled their resources with a commercial producer under the banner of a "rolling premiere." This allows two or more regional theatres and the producer to share the enhanced production costs, thereby reducing each party's financial obligations and risk to the producer's investors.

Commercial Transfer

Once the new work has been fully developed and determined to be commercially viable, the production will transfer to Broadway, West End, tour, or even off-Broadway. The average capitalization of a new Broadway musical is $11–14 million, and the average capitalization of a new Broadway play is $2–4 million. West End capitalizations are often 40–60 percent less than Broadway, and tours are cheaper still. Off-Broadway production budgets typically cap at $1–2 million but are often far less expensive than that. The entire capitalization is at risk through recoupment. All box office grosses are reported weekly (eight performances). Operating expenses, referred to as the "nut," are also calculated weekly. On a weekly basis the box office revenue

The Problem with The Dot

must exceed the nut. The author, director, and designers that have been paid an advance against royalties during the developmental period will receive royalties during the commercial run. Royalties are traditionally calculated from gross box office revenue and are included in the nut. As in any business, when weekly revenue exceeds weekly operating expenses, the production turns a profit. Investors stand in first position and receive 100 percent of the adjusted net profits until such time as they are made whole. Recoupment is traditionally targeted within the first 50 weeks following opening night. Upon investor recoupment, adjusted net profits are split 50–50 between the investors and the producers for the life of the production. The regional theatre(s) who staged the enhanced production is/are considered part of the creative team and will participate in the royalty pool for the life of the show as well. An average-size Broadway theatre can gross $98 million annually at average ticket pricing. Add in premium ticket pricing and annual box office grosses can easily exceed $100 million.[2]

Tours and Foreign Territories

Big money goes to shows that globalize by running productions in multiple countries and tours at the same time. Success for a Broadway show is not measured exclusively by financial performance. Broadway is the threshold to the world. The Broadway brand is so powerful that many domestic tours, and most foreign territories, will only book a show that has played on Broadway; thus, branded as a Broadway musical. A Broadway show will be positioned to gross an additional $80 million annually via tours and foreign territories.[3] Regardless of the initial financial performance on Broadway, investors in the original production participate in the revenue of every licensed production that follows around the world. This participation is in the form of licensing fees paid to the original production, plus right of first refusal to invest in subsequent productions.

2. Paulson and Gelles, "'Hamilton' Inc," para. 8.
3. Paulson and Gelles, "'Hamilton' Inc," para. 12.

Clouds

Publishing

When the commercial production has run its course on Broadway, West End, tours, and all global markets, it moves into the publishing realm. The right to publish the new play or musical is negotiated after the commercial opening with a handful of publishing companies, including Musical Theatre International (MTI), Theatrical Rights Worldwide (TRW), Tams Whitmark, R & H Theatricals, Samuel French, and Dramatists Play Services. Once the property moves into publishing, this allows any educational theatre—elementary school through graduate programs—and regional theatre—the smallest community theatre through the most prominent LORT theatre—to produce the play or musical for a fee plus royalties.

To better understand the economic scope and cultural impact of commercial theatre, consider the following statistics:

Broadway

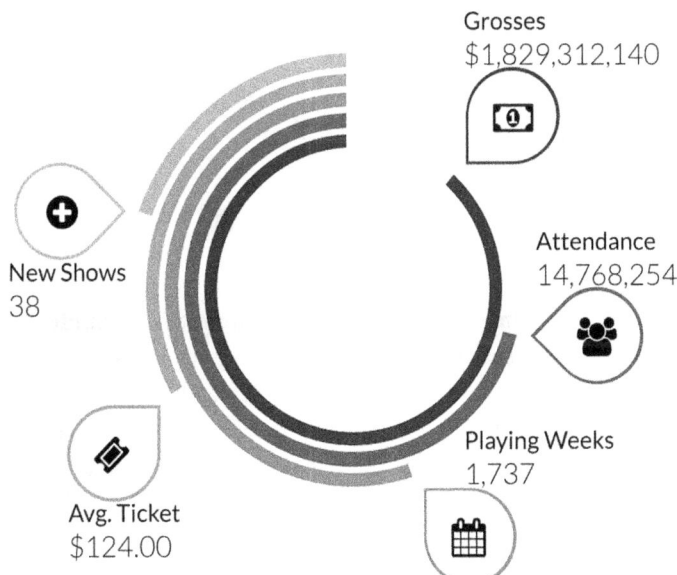

Grosses
$1,829,312,140

New Shows
38

Attendance
14,768,254

Avg. Ticket
$124.00

Playing Weeks
1,737

The Problem with The Dot

An all-time high of 14.8 million people attended a Broadway show during the 2018–2019 Broadway season—more people than attended the seasons of the ten professional New York and New Jersey sports teams *combined* (Mets, Yankees, Rangers, Islanders, Knicks, Liberty, Giants, Jets, Devils, and Nets).[4] With attendance up over the preceding season, that translates into record grosses at the box office to the tune of $1.83 billion.[5]

London's West End

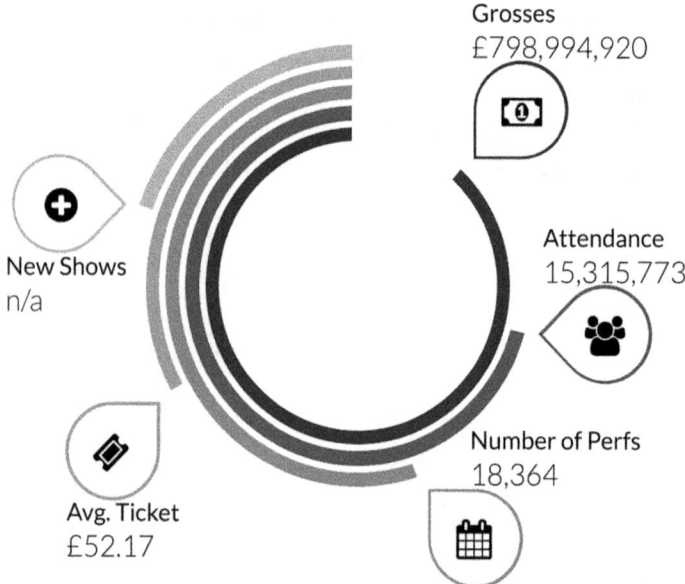

Grosses
£798,994,920

New Shows
n/a

Attendance
15,315,773

Avg. Ticket
£52.17

Number of Perfs
18,364

London's West End was equally successful as its US counterpart during its 2019 season. Attendance was up 3 percent from the previous season, with 15,315,773 people catching a show. Box office grosses totaled £798,994,920 (up 4.3 percent compared to the 2018 season), with more than 80 percent of the available seats filled for the 18,364 performances.[6]

> 4. Hauser, *Demographics of the Broadway Audience*, 5.
> 5. Hauser and Lanier, *Broadway's Economic Contribution*.
> 6. Wax, "2019 Box Office Figures," lines 8–13.

Broadway: US Tours

Eighteen-and-a-half million people across 200 cities attended a touring Broadway production during the 2018–2019 season. The touring season grossed $1.6 billion and contributed a cumulative $3.8 billion to the metropolitan areas that host the shows.[7]

West End: UK Tours

Nearly 19 million people throughout the United Kingdom attended a touring West End production during the 2018 season. The touring season grossed £509,567,967 (up 8.4 percent compared to the 2017 season) with more than 61 percent of the available seats filled for the 44,237 performances.[8]

Cultural and Economic Impact to the Global Theatrical Ecosystem

Christian investors, particularly evangelicals, have not embraced theatre with the same fervor as film. The Hollywood film industry touts larger budgets and opening weekend press releases, but this masks the fact that film has a narrower reach and smaller financial upside, erroneously leading Christian financiers away from commercial theatre investment. Clearly, the statistics form a compelling case for the culture-creating power of the commercial theatre, but how does theatre compare to film in head-to-head competition? Perhaps Disney is the only company that can answer this question definitively:

> Disney's best-selling property has nothing to do with a galaxy far, far away. In fact, it's not even a film. This year, the House of Mouse is celebrating the 20th anniversary of *The Lion King* on Broadway. The duration of the run is impressive enough—most musicals last a year or less,

---

7. Broadway League, "Touring Broadway Facts," lines 1–6.
8. Wax and Allan, "2018 Box Office Figures," para. 5.

The Problem with The Dot

with just a few lucky ones hitting it big. But the real eye-popper is the show's global box office. Including the take from international productions and tours, Disney reps confirmed that: '*The Lion King* has grossed just under $8.1 billion.' Yes, that's a *b*.' That number makes it the highest-grossing entertainment property in history, by a significant margin. The next biggest is *Phantom of The Opera*, with $6 billion. The biggest film is *Avatar*, at just (just!) $2.8 billion. In more Disney-centric terms: *The Lion King has made more money than all of the Star Wars films combined.*[9]

It's important to note that the grosses referenced in the article are for box office revenue only, not including merchandise, cast recordings, and, most importantly, the animated film version of *The Lion King*. Keep in mind that the musical is still running and grosses are still climbing.

Finances are one thing, but what about the people who have been influenced by this global culture-creating art? That number is even more impressive: 92.4 million people have seen *The Lion King* in 20 countries, in eight languages, and every continent, except Antarctica.[10] The tendency may be to dismiss *The Lion King* as an outlier. *Avatar* long held the title for highest grossing film of all time but recently was eclipsed by *Avengers: Endgame*. Both films have earned just over $2.7 billion at the box office. However, if *Avengers: Endgame* is the ceiling of the film industry at $2.797 billion,[11] then consider the following musical theatre productions that have exceeded Hollywood's ceiling:

- *Phantom of the Opera* (1986) grossed $6.2 billion globally and has been seen by 140 million people in 35 countries and in 15 languages.[12]

---

9. Seymour, "Over the Last 20 Years," paras. 4–8.
10. Lion King International Tour, "About the International Tour," para. 8.
11. Box Office Mojo, "Avengers: Endgame."
12. *Phantom of the Opera*, "Facts & Figures," para. 2.

- *Wicked* (2003) grossed $4 billion and has been seen by more than 50 million people in 14 countries and in six languages.[13]
- *CATS* (1981) grossed $2.87 billion[14] and has been seen by more than 73 million people in more than 30 countries and in 15 languages.[15]
- *Les Misérables* (1980) grossed $2.71 billion[16] and has been seen by more than 70 million people in 45 countries and in 22 languages.[17]

That's the top five highest-grossing musicals, but consider all the musicals that have grossed more than $1 billion:

Billion-Dollar Musicals

The Lion King	1997	Has grossed $8.1 billion globally; been seen by 92.4 million people in 20 countries and eight languages; played on every continent except Antarctica;[18] started with an original Broadway production budget of $20 million;[19] and is still playing.
Phantom of the Opera	1986	Has grossed $6.2 billion globally; been seen by 140 million people in 35 countries and 15 languages;[20] started with an original Broadway production budget of $8 million;[21] and is still playing.

13. Cox, "'Wicked' Hits $1 Billion," paras. 3–4.
14. "Money, Money, Money," para. 2.
15. *CATS* North American tour homepage, https://ustour.catsthemusical.com.
16. "Money, Money, Money," para. 2.
17. Clements, "Les Mis," para 11.
18. Seymour, "Over the Last 20 Years," paras. 4–8.
19. "From Riches to Ragtime," para. 5.
20. Phantom of the Opera, "Facts & Figures," para. 2.
21. Ehren, "Broadway Phantom Facts and Figures," para. 6.

The Problem with The Dot

Billion-Dollar Musicals

Wicked	2004	Has grossed $4 billion globally; been seen by 50 million people in 14 countries and six languages;[22] started with an original Broadway production budget of $14 million;[23] and is still playing.
Mamma Mia	1999	Has grossed $4 billion globally; been seen by 65 million people in 16 languages;[24] and started with an original Broadway production budget of $10 million.[25]
CATS	1981	Has grossed $2.87 billion globally;[26] been seen by 73 million people in 30 countries and 15 languages;[27] and started with an original Broadway production budget of $4 million.[28]
Les Misérables	1980	Has grossed $2.71 billion globally;[29] been seen by 70 million people in 52 countries and 22 languages;[30] started with an original £1.14 million West End budget; and is still playing.

22. Cox, "'Wicked' Hits $1 Billion," paras. 3–4.
23. Barnes, "How 'Wicked' Cast Its Spell," para. 1.
24. Judy Craymer Productions, "Press Centre: Facts & Figures," paras. 1–2.
25. Ehren, "Money, Money, Money," para. 1.
26. "Money, Money, Money," para. 2.
27. *CATS* North American tour homepage, https://ustour.catsthemusical.com.
28. Morfoot, "Producer Says Cats Could Recoup," para. 5
29. "Money, Money, Money," para. 2.
30. Clements, "Les Mis," para 11.

Clouds

Billion-Dollar Musicals

Jersey Boys	2004	Has grossed $2 billion globally; been seen by 25 million people;[31] started with an original Broadway production budget of $7.8 million; and is still playing.[32]
Beauty and the Beast	1993	Has grossed $1.7 billion globally; been seen by 35 million people in 13 countries;[33] and started with an original Broadway production budget of $11.9 million.[34]
Miss Saigon	1989	Has grossed $1.64 billion globally;[35] been seen by 34 million people in 29 countries and 15 languages;[36] and started with an original Broadway production budget of $10.9 million.[37]
Starlight Express	1984	Has grossed $1.2 billion globally; been seen by 20 million people;[38] started with an original West End production budget of £2.25 million; and is still playing.[39]
Hamilton	2015	Has grossed $1.02 billion globally;[40] been seen by 60 million people in 16 languages; started with an original Broadway production budget of $12.5 million; and is still playing.[41]

31. Gans, "Jersey Boys Will End," para. 5.
32. Ng, "'Jersey Boys' Has Been a Windfall," para. 16.
33. "Money, Money, Money," para. 2.
34. Witchel, "Is Disney the Newest Broadway Baby?," para. 10.
35. "Money, Money, Money," para. 2.
36. Davies, "Behind the Scenes," para. 5.
37. McKinley, "'Miss Saigon' to End," para. 5.
38. *Starlight Express* homepage, http://www.starlightexpress.com.
39. Fandom, "1984 London Production," para. 30.
40. Chmielewski, "Lin-Manuel Miranda's 'Hamilton,'" para. 3.
41. Paulson and Gelles, "'Hamilton' Inc.," para. 3.

The Problem with The Dot

Buttoning up the head-to-head comparison, it must be emphasized that the 11 highest-grossing musicals of all time have each breached the $1 billion threshold, with the top 7 grossing more than $2 billion, while only 5 films in all of film history have crossed the $2 billion threshold: *Avengers: Endgame* ($2.8 billion),[42] *Avatar* ($2.7 billion),[43] *Titanic* ($2.2 billion),[44] *Star Wars: The Force Awakens* ($2.06 billion),[45] and *Avengers: Infinity War* ($2.04 billion).[46] Film, unlike theatre, offers the potential for fast returns, but often sacrifices long-term cultural influence in the process. *Forbes* offered this commentary on the fifth-year anniversary of *Avatar*'s release:

> *Avatar* earned rave reviews, went on to become by far the highest-grossing movie of all time, and won several Oscars. It then almost immediately vanished from the popular zeitgeist, leaving almost no pop culture impact to speak of. It did not inspire a passionate following, or a deluge of multimedia spin-offs that has kept the brand alive over the last five years. Few today will even admit to liking it, and its overall effect on the culture at large is basically non-existent. It came, it crushed all long-term box office records, and it vanished almost without a trace.[47]

While two of the highest grossing films have all but faded into film history, 10 of the top 11 highest-grossing musicals are currently performing 20 and 30 years later on Broadway (New York City), West End (London), Paris, Shanghai, Hamburg, Tokyo, Madrid, the Netherlands, Singapore, Korea, Taiwan, Australia, South Africa, Brazil, Denmark, Budapest, Oslo, and Prague, to name only a few; in addition to US and world tours. For those who desire cultural influence spanning generations, coupled with the potential for long-term passive income derived from an initial

---

42. Box Office Mojo, "Avengers: Endgame."
43. Box Office Mojo, "Avatar."
44. Box Office Mojo, "Titanic."
45. Box Office Mojo, "Star Wars: Episode VII."
46. Box Office Mojo, "Avengers: Infinity War."
47. Mendelson, "Five Years Ago," para. 1.

investment, then commercial theatre provides a much better opportunity than even the biggest film franchises.

For an investor, isolating global grosses only tells half the story. How do grosses compare to production costs for both film and theatre? Research reveals 46 films have grossed more than $1 billion globally for cumulative global lifetime grosses of $60.6 billion.[48] The problem is the production costs. These tentpole[49] films start at $60 million and quickly escalate to north of $300 million, with an average production budget of $200 million.[50] The cumulative total investment for all 46 films was $9.2 billion (not including marketing budgets). Had an investor financed all 46 films, then he or she would have received a 658.79 percent return on investment (ROI).[51]

Billion-Dollar Films[52]

Title	Year	Worldwide Box Office Gross Revenue (in millions)	Reported Production Budget (in millions)
Avengers: Endgame	2019	$2,797	$356
Avatar	2009	$2,789	$237
Titanic	1997	$2,187	$200
Star Wars: The Force Awakens	2015	$2,068	$245

    48. IMDb, "Billion-Dollar Film Club."
    49. *Merriam-Webster.com Dictionary*, s.v. "tentpole," https://www.merriam-webster.com/dictionary/tentpole.
    50. IMDb, "Billion-Dollar Film Club."
    51. Calculated from the totals in the table "Billion Dollar Films."
    52. IMDb, "Billion-Dollar Film Club," unless otherwise noted.

The Problem with The Dot

Billion-Dollar Films[52]

Avengers: Infinity War	2018	$2,048	$500[53]
Jurassic World	2015	$1,671	$150
The Lion King	2019	$1,656	$250[54]
The Avengers	2012	$1,518	$220
Furious 7	2015	$1,516	$190
Frozen II	2019	$1,438	$150
Avengers: Age of Ultron	2015	$1,405	$250
Black Panther	2018	$1,346	$200[55]
Harry Potter and the Deathly Hallows Part 2	2011	$1,341	$250[56]
Star Wars: The Last Jedi	2017	$1,332	$317[57]
Jurassic World: Fallen Kingdom	2018	$1,309	$170
Frozen	2013	$1,276	$150
Beauty and the Beast	2017	$1,263	$60
Incredibles 2	2018	$1,242	$200[58]
The Fate of the Furious	2016	$1,236	$250

53. Hensley, "Dan Cathy," para. 23.
54. Giardina, "Lion King' 'Virtual Production,'" para. 7.
55. McClintock, "Box-Office Milestone," para. 6.
56. Frankel, "Get Ready for the Biggest 'Potter,'" para. 11.
57. McDonald, *2017 Feature Film Study*, 15.
58. Sakoui and Patton, "'Incredibles 2' Smashes Record," para. 9.

Clouds

Billion-Dollar Films[52]

Iron Man 3	2013	$1,214	$200
Minions	2015	$1,159	$74
Captain America: Civil War	2016	$1,153	$250
Aquaman	2018	$1,148	$200[59]
The Lord of the Rings: The Return of the King	2003	$1,142	$94
Spider-Man: Far from Home	2019	$1,131	$160
Captain Marvel	2019	$1,128	$152
Transformers: Dark of the Moon	2011	$1,123	$195
Skyfall	2012	$1,108	$200
Transformers: Age of Extinction	2014	$1,104	$210
The Dark Knight Rises	2012	$1,084	$250
Joker	2019	$1,073	$55
Toy Story 4	2019	$1,073	$200
Star Wars: Episode 9 —The Rise of Skywalker	2019	$1,067	$275[60]
Pirates of the Caribbean: Dead Man's Chest	2006	$1,066	$225
Toy Story 3	2010	$1,066	$200

59. Rubin, "Box Office: 'Aquaman,'" para. 6.
60. Brueggemann, "'Star Wars: The Rise of Skywalker,'" para. 16.

The Problem with The Dot

Billion-Dollar Films[52]

Film	Year	Gross	Budget
Rogue One: A Star Wars Story	2016	$1,056	$200
Aladdin	2019	$1,050	$183
Pirates of the Caribbean: On Stranger Tides	2011	$1,045	$250
Despicable Me 3	2017	$1,034	$80
Jurassic Park	1993	$1,029	$63
Finding Dory	2016	$1,028	$175[61]
Stars Wars: Episode 1 —The Phantom Menace	1999	$1,027	$115
Alice in Wonderland	2014	$1,025	$200
Zootopia	2016	$1,023	$150[62]
The Hobbit: An Unexpected Journey	2012	$1,017	$315[63]
The Dark Knight	2008	$1,004	$185
TOTALS		$60,615	$9,201

By comparison, commercial theatre would have proven a much better investment strategy. Of the musicals that have each grossed more than $1 billion globally, the cumulative global lifetime grosses is $35.7 billion (and growing). The cumulative total initial investment is $105 million—yes, *million*, with an *m*, and less than the cost of a single tentpole film.[64] More noticeably, commer-

61. McNary, "'Finding Dory' Swimming for Record," para. 9.
62. Barnes, "'Zootopia' Tops the Box Office," para. 2.
63. Masters, "'Hobbit': Inside Peter Jackson," para. 10
64. See the table "Billion Dollar Musicals."

cial theatre production budgets *include* marketing. Had an investor financed all 11 musicals, then the commercial theatre investor would have made a 33,898.83 percent ROI. Furthermore, the commercial theatre investor is still earning passive income from every single theatre production still running.

My experience in capitalizing commercial theatre indicates Christian investors are more actively engaged with Christian film financing while shunning theatre investment opportunities. These investment decisions aren't nearly as rewarding. The cumulative global lifetime grosses of the top 13 Christian films is $2.89 billion to date. The cumulative total investment is $703 million.[65] Had an investor participated in every one of the top 13 Christian films, he or she would have invested $598 million more and earned $32.8 billion less than he or she would have by investing in the top 11 grossing musicals.

Top-Grossing Christian Films

Title	Year	Worldwide Box Office Gross Revenue (in millions)	Reported Production Budget (in millions)
Narnia: The Lion, The Witch and the Wardrobe[66]	2005	$745	$180
The Passion of the Christ[67]	2004	$612	$30
Narnia: Prince Caspian[68]	2008	$419	$225

65. See the table "Billion Dollar Films."
66. Box Office Mojo, "Chronicles of Narnia: The Lion, the Witch and the Wardrobe."
67. "The Passion of the Christ,".
68. Box Office Mojo, "Chronicles of Narnia: Prince Caspian."

The Problem with The Dot

Top-Grossing Christian Films

Narnia: The Voyage of the Dawn Treader[69]	2010	$415	$155
Heaven Is for Real[70]	2014	$101	$12
The Shack	2017	$97[71]	$20[72]
I Can Only Imagine[73]	2018	$86	$7
The Star[74]	2017	$84	$20
Miracles from Heaven[75]	2016	$74	$13
War Room[76]	2015	$73	$3
Son of God	2014	$72[77]	$22[78]
God's Not Dead[79]	2014	$65	$2
Breakthrough[80]	2019	$50	$14
TOTALS		$2,892	$703

    69. Box Office Mojo, "Chronicles of Narnia: The Voyage of the Dawn Treader."
    70. Box Office Mojo, "Heaven Is for Real,".
    71. Box Office Mojo, "Shack."
    72. Lang, "Box Office: 'Logan' Slicing," para. 6.
    73. Box Office Mojo, "I Can Only Imagine."
    74. Box Office Mojo, "Star."
    75. Box Office Mojo, "Miracles from Heaven."
    76. Box Office Mojo, "War Room."
    77. Box Office Mojo, "Son of God."
    78. Somers, "In 'Son of God,'" para. 9.
    79. Box Office Mojo, "God's Not Dead."
    80. Box Office Mojo, "Breakthrough."

Clouds

These investors are operating on the false premise that film has a larger global cultural presence than theatre. I will concede that a studio's tentpole opening weekend will have an initial global impact that exceeds the opening weekend capabilities of theatre. However, after opening weekend, even tentpole films begin an often quick descent into obscurity.[81] Hollywood's global impact and revenue must be realized in a narrow window of opportunity. Independent films are not exempt from this revenue cycle, and the effects are more pronounced. By contrast, Broadway is the threshold to the world and is only the beginning of the revenue cycle. Commercial theatre's business model is built for long-term sustained success that outpaces the number of people reached as well as the gross revenue of even the most successful films studied. Why modify investment strategies to include commercial theatre? If the investor of faith hopes to be altruistic while simultaneously positioning for the maximum return, then the bigger bang for the buck is undoubtedly commercial theatre, where production budgets are far more manageable and grosses can exceed even the most successful film franchises.

The perception is that investing in Broadway is riskier than investing in the stock market. To dispel this myth, I researched 12 Broadway seasons beginning with the 2007–2008 season to establish a baseline prior to the Great Recession, and concluding with the 2018–2019 season—the final full season before COVID-19 abruptly ended the 2019–2020 season and disrupted the following 2020–2021 season. The research that follows is raw data from the Broadway League that I have collated over a number of years.

During this time, 170 musicals and 248 plays, for a total of 418 productions, opened on Broadway, excluding special engagements.[82] I tracked every available data point for all 418 productions, including, but not limited to, length of run, percentage of theater capacity, percentage of gross box office revenue, admission prices, and top ticket prices (VIP tickets). On average, 14 musicals open each

---

81. Mendelson, "Five Years Ago."

82. Special engagements are often limited to a single performance or limited runs, typically mounted during the holiday season.

season with a production budget of $11,049,451. Plays are much less expensive to produce, which accounts for the 21 plays that opened with an average production budget of $2,916,247. Over 12 seasons, audiences filled theaters to 80 percent capacity for musicals and 77 percent capacity for plays. Tickets to a musical average $84 whereas plays carry a $79 average ticket price. Broadway reports grosses weekly based on 8 performances. The business model is simple in concept: weekly box office revenue must exceed weekly operating expenses. Average weekly operating expenses tally up to $705,947 for a musical and $376,619 for a play. Given the average capacity, ticket pricing and weekly operating expenses, musicals recoup their production budget in 48 weeks and 4 days, while plays take 15 weeks and 4 days. The length of time for recoupment support the parameters of the investment offerings. Musicals are traditionally open-ended engagements that are designed to recoup within the first year but will run as long as they are profitable. Plays, on the other hand, are typically 16-week limited engagements with an above-the-title star actor attached. The star actor's schedule will often determine the length of run and whether the run can be extended. The average length of run for a play is 16 weeks and 5 days, while the average length of run for a musical is 52 weeks and 1 day. During the past 12 seasons, 19 percent of all musicals successfully recouped all production costs and 24 percent of all plays successfully recouped.

The preceding averages don't paint a completely accurate picture for the independent investor. Unlike independent productions, Disney, as a corporation, rarely reports recoupment and production costs, reserving such announcements for only the most prominent success stories.[83] Additionally, the Lincoln Center Theatre, Manhattan Theatre Club (MTC), Roundabout Theatre Company, and 2nd Stage are all non-profit theatre companies designated as Broadway theatres with Tony Award eligibility, but none report production costs or recoupment. In general, neither Disney nor the non-profit theatre companies offer investment opportunities for independent producers. For the purposes of this comparative analysis, I

---

83. See the table "Billion Dollar Musicals" for *The Lion King* and *Beauty and the Beast* information.

Clouds

removed all Disney and non-profit theatre productions from the 12-season study in order to compare the performance of 327 "investable productions" to the performance of the S&P 500 Index over the same 12 seasons. I assumed all capital is expended within each season/year and that all returns are redeemed at the end of each run/season/year. Annual returns for both Broadway and the S&P 500 are not compounded. Annual investment capital for the S&P is determined by the per-season total investment capital for Broadway productions. This analysis is exclusive to Broadway gross box office revenue only. There is no consideration of additional domestic productions, foreign territories, domestic, and global tours, or merchandising revenue streams.

S&P 500 Index Results by Year[84]

Year	Initial Investment	Profit/Loss	Ending Capital	S&P 500 Return
2008	$126,651,190.48	-$48,748,043.21	$77,903,147.26	-38.49%
2009	$176,301,785.71	$41,342,768.75	$217,644,554.46	23.45%
2010	$176,301,785.71	$22,531,368.21	$198,833,153.93	12.78%
2011	$174,600,000.00	$0.00	$174,600,000.00	0.00%
2012	$183,960,000.00	$24,669,036.00	$208,629,036.00	13.41%
2013	$161,944,615.38	$47,935,606.15	$209,880,221.54	29.60%
2014	$163,393,846.15	$18,610,559.08	$182,004,405.23	11.39%
2015	$176,440,000.00	-$1,288,012.00	$175,151,988.00	-0.73%
2016	$204,900,000.00	$19,547,460.00	$224,447,460.00	9.54%
2017	$249,966,666.67	$48,543,526.67	$298,510,193.33	19.42%
2018	$119,200,000.00	-$7,438,080.00	$111,761,920.00	-6.24%
2019	$197,641,608.39	$57,078,896.50	$254,720,504.90	28.88%

84. MacroTrends, "S&P 500 Historical Annual Returns."

The Problem with The Dot

Broadway Investment Results by Season

Season	Initial Investment	Gross Box Office Revenue	Weekly Operating Expenses	Ending Capital	Season Return
2007–8	$126,651,190.48	$338,318,165.00	-$343,785,552.25	-$5,467,387.25	-104.32%
2008–9	$176,301,785.71	$691,146,376.00	-$639,310,017.03	$51,836,358.97	-70.60%
2009–10	$176,301,785.71	$536,568,015.00	-$449,779,313.05	$86,788,701.95	-50.77%
2010–11	$174,600,000.00	$1,059,360,469.00	-$612,034,933.13	$447,325,535.87	156.20%
2011–12	$183,960,000.00	$633,277,993.00	-$406,197,919.27	$227,080,073.73	23.44%
2012–13	$161,944,615.38	$995,344,652.00	-$699,487,177.07	$295,857,474.93	82.69%
2013–14	$163,393,846.15	$790,788,552.00	-$642,354,548.28	$148,434,003.72	-9.16%
2014–15	$176,440,000.00	$600,756,171.00	-$472,656,204.13	$128,099,966.87	-27.40%
2015–16	$204,900,000.00	$1,400,484,449.00	-$770,320,036.58	$630,164,412.42	207.55%
2016–17	$249,966,666.67	$1,146,405,550.00	-$758,474,364.46	$387,931,185.54	55.19%
2017–18	$119,200,000.00	$624,248,790.00	-$325,481,027.97	$298,767,762.03	150.64%
2018–19	$197,641,608.39	$748,686,299.00	-$486,281,628.22	$262,404,670.78	32.77%

Clouds

The analysis is revealing on many levels. Over the 12 seasons, an investor who participated in every "investible production" capitalized 148 musicals and 179 plays for a total investment of $2.1 billion. These productions have grossed $9.5 billion at the box office and incurred $6.6 billion in weekly operating expenses. Of the 327 productions, 27 percent have recouped and 6 are still running. In total, the productions have returned $3 billion in net profits—a 40-percent ROI, or 2.85-percent annualized ROI.

Theatre ROI

Total Capital Invested	$2,111,301,498.50
Total Shows Capitalized	327
Total Shows That Announced Recoupment	88
Announced Success Rate	26.91%
Total Playing Weeks	1,0837
Total Gross Box Office Revenue	$9,565,385,481.00
Total Weekly Operating Expenses	-$6,606,162,721.44
Total 12-season Profit	$2,959,222,759.56
Broadway 12-season Return	40.16%
Annualized ROI	2.85%
Standard Deviation	97.40%
Sharpe Ratio[85]	0.0293

85. Hargrave, "How to Use the Sharpe Ratio," para. 1.

The Problem with The Dot

The same $2.1 billion investment on the S&P 500 would return a $222 million net profit. This is a 10-percent ROI or .84-percent annualized ROI over the same 12-year period.

S&P 500 ROI

Total Capital Invested	$2,111,301,498.50
Total Profit/Loss	$2,334,086,584.65
Total 12-year Profit	$222,785,086.15
S&P 500 12-year Return	10.55%
Annualized ROI	0.84%
Standard Deviation	18.68%
Sharpe Ratio[1]	0.0449

One may expect a high-risk venture like commercial theatre to yield a high return. Yet the analysis also supports classic portfolio theory, in which exposure to risk is minimized when investing across the entire market.

This entire chapter on commercial theatre is meant to: (a) introduce a basic understanding of how commercial theatrical productions are brought to market; (b) diminish the notion that film is more financially lucrative than theatre; (c) persuade Christian film investors who desire cultural impact and ROI to consider theatre as a viable option that outperforms Christian film in both objectives; and (d) demonstrate that broad investment in the commercial theatre market over an extended timeframe reduces risk and outperforms more traditional investment methods.

In summary, commercial theatre is a niche industry, global in scale, with two major markets—Broadway and West End—that

---

1. Hargrave, "How to Use the Sharpe Ratio," para. 1.

Clouds

have combined annual grosses of more than $4 billion, with an audience of more than 65 million.

Understanding commercial theatre, as well as educational and regional theatre, is foundational to embracing the next chapter. The call to action presents a holistic approach for global regenerative culture-making through the theatre artist care initiatives of CITA and a comprehensive plan for theatre investment with The Repertoire Fund.

The Theatrical Ecosystem

A Call to Action

A LOT OF INFORMATION has been presented and it seems a recap may set the stage for the final call to action. This book has outlined the four components of the theatrical ecosystem and corrective action needed for each.

Illustration by Maggie B. French

The Theatrical Ecosystem

Headwaters: Theology and Theatre

The headwaters are the source that influences every downstream component of the theatrical ecosystem. The primal source is Holy Scripture, and beyond the primal source are the relatively new headwaters of theology and theatre.

- Theologians and artists of faith must continue the fairly recent collaboration that advances the theological and academic link between Scripture and theatrical arts.

- Theologians and artists must educate current and future clergy as well as other Christian influencers regarding the necessity of regenerative culture care on a global scale through the theatrical arts.

- Artists of faith need theologians and clergy to support their efforts to abolish the segregation of sacred art and secular art, thereby extending their work beyond The Dot.

Lakes: Educational Theatre

The lakes of educational theatre, with their relatively safe waters, are where the next generation of artists coalesces for education and training within the theatrical ecosystem.

- Christian education leadership must embrace theatre as a viable mission field and career path for the next generation of artists.

- Training the next generation of artists starts as early as secondary school, and theatre's importance should be embraced in Christian elementary, middle, and high schools, and not coopted as simply a competitive marketing tool for the recruitment of potential students and their families.

- Thirteen million US students who participate in theatre are the next generation of artists.

- The role of undergraduate degrees is critical to the long-term sustainability of the theatrical ecosystem. Christian individuals and organizations must create and/or fund theatre scholarships that provide access to the best universities and conservatories for the next generation of artists.
- There are 20 million post-secondary students in the United States.
- There are 1,873 theatre programs in the United States training the next generation of artists.
- These students and programs are largely ignored or, worse, substandard on Christian college campuses.
- Graduate programs are where the next generation of arts leadership is formed. Christian universities must offer better terminal degree programs, grow and strengthen the alumni associations, and, most importantly, establish conservatories that are competitive with flagship programs worldwide.

Oceans: Regional Theatre

Within the theatrical ecosystem, new theatre graduates and seasoned professionals merge in the ocean of regional theatre, which cultivates culture within local communities.

- There are an estimated 1,850 professional non-profit regional theatres in the United States that cumulatively contribute more than $2 billion to local economies.
- Regional theatres influence local culture by attracting an audience of 31 million adults and children nationally.
- The role of regional theatre within any given community is threefold:
    1. Engage the community
    2. Educate the community
    3. Entertain the community

The Theatrical Ecosystem

- Within the broader term of regional theatre are several subsets, including theatre for young audience organizations, applied theatre companies, and Christian theatre companies. All subsets serve as entry points for artists of faith, but the vast majority of work in regional theatre is not found in the subsets.
- Regional theatre in a formal relationship with a university, while somewhat rare, is not unprecedented. This type of partnership is nonexistent on any Christian university campus. This must change as the benefits far exceed the challenges of shared resources.

Clouds: Commercial Theatre

Similar to environmental ecosystems, commercial theatre can be likened to the formation of clouds that replenish the entire ecosystem, with the potential to reshape the entire theatrical ecosystem.

Commercial theatre is derived from the theatrical ecosystem:

- Discovery of a new work often transpires in educational or regional theatre.
- Development of new work always takes place in regional theatre and occasionally in educational theatre.
- Out-of-town tryouts are where the commercial projects are brought to life, almost always in regional theatre.
- Commercial productions, including foreign and domestic tours, are the financial exploitation of the new work around the world.
- Publishing is when the work replenishes the balance of the theatrical ecosystem and becomes available to all theatres around the world.
- Commercial theatre cultivates culture on every continent of our planet, excluding Antarctica, creating life, and quality of life, for more than six million people, with cumulative box office grosses exceeding $36 billion dollars.

- Each component of the theatrical ecosystem strengthens the case for a long-term, holistic approach to the care and cultivation of global culture through the theatrical ecosystem.

This necessitates an immediate two-part call to action: a) for all those committed to regenerative culture-making to join CITA; and b) for investors to participate in the capitalization of The Repertoire Fund,[1] a theatre investment collective.

In 1987, a group of Christians organized CITA[2] out of concern that Christian theatre artists were laboring in relative isolation from one another. CITA's first objective was to make available an ongoing network of conferences and printed materials to these artists. CITA's membership and influence grew, along with the burgeoning Willow Creek Community Church drama ministry, which peaked in the early 2000s. The maturation of e-commerce and social media networking conspired against CITA's original intent. In 2011, CITA reimagined its focus and created trilateral initiatives: Applied Theatre, Emerging Artist/New Works, and CITA to the Nations. Of those, two initiatives flourished for another season until the Applied Theatre Center became a separate entity in the summer of 2018. In January 2020, CITA relaunched with a refined purpose: "CITA cultivates environments that empower and sustain all Christians in Theatre Arts." This refocusing strategically engages the theatrical ecosystem through the following areas.

CITA: Theatre and Theology cultivates the relationship between theatre and theology for the formation of healthy Christian theatre artists. CITA accomplishes this mission through a four-part strategy:

1. Reinforcing the symbiotic nature of theatre and theology as well as the Christian's involvement in theatre arts
2. Deepening the Christian theatre artists' connection to their faith and theatrical communities

---

1. See https://www.therepertoirefund.com/.
2. See https://cita.org/home.

The Theatrical Ecosystem

3. Supporting the formation of faithful and mature Christian theatre artists

4. Encouraging Christian theatre artists to approach their craft as a formative work of art

CITA: Educational Theatre empowers the next generation of Christian theatre artists to excel in their calling and career. CITA accomplishes this mission through a four-part strategy:

1. Infusing students' education with a Christian worldview
2. Providing students with platforms for the development of their craft
3. Connecting students with the next step in their training and career
4. Introducing students to Christian professionals in their field

CITA: Professional Theatre sustains Christian theatre artists who engage in regenerative culture making. CITA accomplishes this mission through a four-part strategy:

1. Providing professional development and continuing education for Christian theatre artists within their field
2. Connecting Christian theatre artists to their professional communities
3. Establishing an international network of Christian theatre artists within the industry
4. Helping Christian theatre artists rejoin the global conversation

CITA supports each initiative with services and events designed specifically for each component of the theatrical ecosystem. Examples of these include weekly communal reading of Scripture, reconciliation- and student-focused webinars and podcasts, CITA Conclave, the Secondary Theatre Festival, the One Act Play Festival, New Play Conference, New Musical Theatre Conference, and the Christian Theatre Intensive.

developmental pipeline while creating an additional revenue stream.

3. Integrate technology for monetized digital distribution of The Repertoire Fund's stories thereby creating additional revenue streams while simultaneously building a global audience anticipating the live stage experience.

4. Reduce risk by producing a curated portfolio of stories at regular intervals over an extended period across a wide range of global mediums.

Story Selection Criteria

The Repertoire Fund will produce stories that meet the following criteria:

- *Good*: Is the script well written? Is the plot well structured? Are the characters well developed and authentic? Are the six elements of drama all accounted for and properly balanced within the script? Does the story adhere to the rules of the genre?

- *Beautiful*: Does the story evoke an appropriate emotional response? Does the story inspire me to action? Do I want to experience it again? Do I develop a connection with the characters? Does the music stick with me or move me emotionally? Do the costumes, set, lighting, sound, etc. bring me joy? Do I feel better for having spent time with the story? Does this art breathe oxygen into my soul?

- *True*: Does the story reveal truth about our human condition? Does the story reveal objective truth about interpersonal, intrapersonal, intragroup, or intergroup conflict? Does the story reveal truth about my own relational or spiritual welfare? Does the truth of this story help me better understand and develop more empathy for those different from me? Am I inspired to be a better human being for having experienced this story?

- *Commercial*: Does this story have theatrical mass market appeal? Does this story include universal themes sufficient to perform well theatrically in foreign markets? Can this story be adapted to and exploited in mediums other than theatre?

Healing a degenerative culture will require Christian artists and financiers, working in concert through CITA and The Repertoire Fund, to cultivate and care for local and global culture. For those who are artists, this means creating formative works of art, beautiful stories for the stage, for beauty is oxygen to a world suffocating in a degenerative culture. For those with wealth, a portion of that wealth should be invested strategically in The Repertoire Fund, yielding generational global culture care, while realizing an above-average, risk-adjusted return on investment.

The theatrical ecosystem is a delicate system as intricately designed by God as any in the physical world, and it has been neglected for too long. Together, artists of faith and Christian financiers can be faithful to the original mandate and restore the Garden (Gen 2:15) to health by providing regenerative beauty to our global culture for generations to come.

Afterword

THE READER HAS JUST taken a boat ride through Bruce Long's navigable ecosystem, a journey that outlines the sources of the present state of the art of not only the secular but also the Christian subcultural theatrical waterscape. The dams or choke points that would impede the free flow of ideas, organizations, and the plays are artfully articulated in this book. These include a parochialism of the believer towards the arts themselves, which carries over into a neglect on the part of the churches, the schools, both secondary and collegiate, and finally into the transformational regional and commercial ventures that sparsely populate this nation's theatrical offerings.

This afterword is written during the COVID-19 burgeoning outbreak, which began in January of 2020 and which continues into the publication of this book. To complete the metaphor, the ports are closed, the boats anchored or in dry dock, and the source has turned to a trickle. Sports events are played to empty stadiums, and theatre offerings, such as the musical *Hamilton*, are presented exclusively as video fare. Is theatre in for a permanent decline? Is theatre itself, which relies on and is defined by live audiences and live actors, to be relegated to the virtual swamps of digital outpourings? I don't think so. The pandemic is going to end. And certainly, like the aftermath of a hurricane with its onslaught of high tides and water damage, the theatrical landscape will be littered with wreckage. So, as the pieces are put back together, as theatres attempt to re-establish their worth in the cultural and educational

Afterword

communities in which they were founded, what better time to redefine their purpose, their vision, and their relevancy than by considering Bruce Long's *The Problem with the Dot*. One doesn't wade through this book, like in the still waters or the shallows; instead, think in terms of cavorting, of splashing, of riding the waves and discovering new possibilities and insights into the particular disciplines in which the reader might be involved. There is going to need to be a rebuilding of the live theatrical experience. What better way to confront the doldrums of personal distancing than to once again celebrate the live immediacy of theatre, whether it be in role-playing efforts in the elementary classroom, or the festive dances that characterize the end of Shakespeare's comedies. Touch is going to be back in big time. The Netflix and Amazon addicts are going to be substituting the remote for "front row, center." Note the ironic definition of this plastic channel changer as "having very little connection with or relationship to" intimacy and relationship between people.

The highly charged and optimistic expression of this resurgence of a cultural art form is revealed in Bruce Long's treatment of The Repertoire Fund, probably the flagship of his cumulative redemptive vision. It represents a trickle-down approach that starts with the mission of identifying and producing "a diversified portfolio of high-quality commercial theatre stories that foster the good, the beautiful, and the true in global audiences while realizing an above-average, risk-adjusted return on investment." It's exciting. It's possible. So, can the reader dare to become a part of this vision into a "wild dedication of self to undiscovered waters, and undreamed shores"?[1]

Gillette Elvgren Jr.

---

1. Shakespeare, *The Winter's Tale*, act 4, scene 4.

Bibliography

Abilene Christian University. "Abilene Shakespeare Festival." https://www.acu.edu/on-campus/undergraduate/college-of-arts-and-sciences/theatre-department/abilene-shakespeare-festival.html.
https://www.boxofficemojo.com/title/tt0980970/?ref_=bo_se_r_3.
Balthasar, Hans Urs von. *Theo-Drama: Theological Dramatic Theory*. Translated by Graham Harrison. 5 vols. San Francisco: Ignatius, 1988–98.
Barnes, Brooks. "How 'Wicked' Cast Its Spell." *Wall Street Journal*, October 22, 2005. https://www.wsj.com/articles/SB112994038461876413.
———. "'Zootopia' Tops the Box Office." *New York Times*, March 6, 2016. https://www.nytimes.com/2016/03/07/arts/zootopia-tops-the-box-office.html.
Begbie, Jeremy. *Beholding the Glory: Incarnation Through the Arts*. Grand Rapids: Baker, 2001.
———. *A Peculiar Orthodoxy: Reflections on Theology and the Arts*. Grand Rapids: Baker, 2018.
———. *Redeeming Transcendence in the Arts: Bearing Witness to the Triune God*. Grand Rapids: Eerdmans, 2018.
———. *Sounding the Depths: Theology Through the Arts*. London: SCM, 2002.
Bonhoeffer, Dietrich. *The Cost of Discipleship*. Translated by R. H. Fuller. New York: Touchstone, 1995.
Box Office Mojo. "Avatar." https://www.boxofficemojo.com/release/rl876971521/.
———. "Avengers: Endgame." https://www.boxofficemojo.com/title/tt4154796/.
———. "Avengers: Infinity War." https://www.boxofficemojo.com/title/tt4154756/.
———. "Breakthrough." https://www.boxofficemojo.com/title/tt7083526/?ref_=bo_se_r_1.
———. "The Chronicles of Narnia: Prince Caspian." https://www.boxofficemojo.com/title/tt0499448/?ref_=bo_se_r_2.
———. "The Chronicles of Narnia: The Lion, the Witch and the Wardrobe." https://www.boxofficemojo.com/title/tt0363771/?ref_=bo_se_r_1.
———. "The Chronicles of Narnia: The Voyage of the Dawn Treader." Brook, Peter. *The Empty Space*. Harmondsworth, UK: Penguin, 1968.
———. "God's Not Dead." https://www.boxofficemojo.com/title/tt2528814/?ref_=bo_se_r_1.

Bibliography

———. "Heaven Is for Real." https://www.boxofficemojo.com/title/tt1929263/?ref_=bo_se_r_1.
———. "I Can Only Imagine." https://www.boxofficemojo.com/title/tt6450186/?ref_=bo_se_r_1.
———. "Miracles from Heaven." https://www.boxofficemojo.com/title/tt4257926/?ref_=bo_se_r_1.
———. "The Passion of the Christ." https://www.boxofficemojo.com/title/tt0335345/?ref_=bo_se_r_1.
———. "The Shack." https://www.boxofficemojo.com/title/tt2872518/?ref_=bo_se_r_1.
———. "Son of God." https://www.boxofficemojo.com/title/tt3210686/?ref_=bo_se_r_1.
———. "The Star." https://www.boxofficemojo.com/title/tt4587656/?ref_=bo_se_r_1.
———. "Star Wars: Episode VII—The Force Awakens." https://www.boxofficemojo.com/title/tt2488496/.
———. "Titanic." https://www.boxofficemojo.com/title/tt0120338/?ref_=bo_cso_table_3.
———. "War Room." https://www.boxofficemojo.com/title/tt3832914/?ref_=bo_se_r_1.
The Broadway League. "Statistics—Broadway in NYC." https://www.broadwayleague.com/research/statistics-broadway-nyc/.
———. "Touring Broadway Facts." https://www.broadwayleague.com/research/statistics-touring-broadway/.
Brueggemann, Tom. "'Star Wars: The Rise of Skywalker' Wins $175 Million Box Office, While the Farce Be with 'Cats.'" *IndieWire*, December 23, 2019. https://www.indiewire.com/2019/12/star-wars-the-rise-of-skywalker-175-million-box-office-cats-1202198932/.
Chmielewski, Dawn. "Lin-Manuel Miranda's 'Hamilton' Crashes Broadway's Billion-Dollar Club." *Forbes*, June 8, 2020. https://www.forbes.com/sites/dawnchmielewski/2020/06/08/lin-manuel-mirandas-hamilton-crashes-broadways-billion-dollar-club.
Clements, Carly-Ann. "Les Mis: Everything You Need to Know." Official London Theatre, updated December 19, 2019. https://officiallondontheatre.com/news/les-mis-everything-need-know-111407148/.
Cox, Gordon. "'Wicked' Hits $1 Billion on Broadway Faster than Any Other Show." *Variety*, March 15, 2016. https://variety.com/2016/legit/news/wicked-broadway-sales-1-billion-1201730349/.
Craigo-Snell, Shannon. *The Empty Church: Theater, Theology, and Bodily Hope*. Oxford: Oxford University Press, 2014.
Davies, Serena. "Behind the Scenes of the Record-Breaking New Miss Saigon." *The Telegraph*, May 16, 2014. https://www.telegraph.co.uk/culture/theatre/london-shows/10830164/Behind-the-scenes-of-the-record-breaking-new-Miss-Saigon.html.
Dyrness, William A. *Poetic Theology: God and the Poetics of Everyday Life*. Grand Rapids: Eerdmans, 2010.

Bibliography

Ehren, Christine. "Broadway Phantom Facts and Figures." *Playbill*, January 25, 1998. https://www.playbill.com/article/broadway-phantom-facts-and-figures-com-73047.

———. "Money, Money, Money: Hit Mamma Mia! Recoups Its Investment." *Playbill*, May 29, 2002. https://www.playbill.com/article/money-money-money-hit-mamma-mia-recoups-its-investment-com-106096.

Elvgren, Gillette, Jr. "Can I Hear a Witness? Docu-Drama: A Model for Christian Theatre." *Christianity and the Theatre* 19 (1998).

———. "How Then Shall We Write?" *Christianity and Theatre*, Fall/Winter 2004, 3–11.

———. playwright. *Jairus* (2000) and Willow Creek staff, a full-length musical produced by Willow Creek Community Church. Chicago, April 2000.

———. "The State of the Arts: A Symposium." *IMAGE: A Journal of the Arts and Religion* 22 (1999) 78–80.

———. "Theatrical Conventions: Rediscovering Transcendence in Theatre." *The Creative Spirit* 4.1 (Fall 2004) 40–43.

Fandom. "1984 London Production." *Starlight Express* wiki. https://starlightexpressmusical.fandom.com/wiki/1984_London_production.

Frankel, Daniel. "Get Ready for the Biggest 'Potter' Opening Yet." *The Wrap*, November 17, 2010. https://www.thewrap.com/get-ready-biggest-potter-opening-yet-22607/.

"From Riches to Ragtime." *The Economist*, August 13, 1998. https://www.economist.com/business/1998/08/13/from-riches-to-ragtime.

Fujimura, Makoto. *Culture Care: Reconnecting with Beauty for Our Common Life*. Downers Grove, IL: InterVarsity, 2017.

Gans, Andrew. "Jersey Boys Will End Record-Breaking Broadway Run in January." *Playbill*, September 6, 2016. https://www.playbill.com/article/jersey-boys-will-end-record-breaking-broadway-run-in-january.

Giardina, Carolyn. "'The Lion King' 'Virtual Production' Could Be a Game-Changer for Filmmaking." *The Hollywood Reporter*, July 19, 2019. https://www.hollywoodreporter.com/behind-screen/lion-king-virtual-production-could-be-a-game-changer-filmmaking-1224990.

Hargrave, Marshall. "How to Use the Sharpe Ratio to Analyze Portfolio Risk and Return." Investopedia, August 29, 2020. https://www.investopedia.com/terms/s/sharperatio.asp.

Harris, Max. *Theatre and Incarnation*. London: Palgrave Macmillian, 1990.

Hauser, Karen. *Demographics of the Broadway Audience*. New York: Broadway League, 2019.

Hauser, Karen, and Catherine Lanier. *Broadway's Economic Contribution to New York City*. New York: Broadway League, 2019.

Hensley, Ellie. "Dan Cathy: Pinewood Atlanta Studios Hosting 'Largest Film Production Ever.'" *Atlanta Business Chronicle*, March 1, 2017. http://www.bizjournals.com/atlanta/news/2017/03/01/dan-cathy-pinewood-atlanta-studios-hosting.html.

Bibliography

IMDb. "The Billion-Dollar Film Club: 46 Movies to Reach $1 Billion Worldwide." Last updated February 24, 2020. https://www.imdb.com/list/ls063095038/mediaviewer/rm3587670016.

Johnson, Todd. "Doing God's Story: Theatre, Christian Initiation, and Being Human Together." In *Theatrical Theology: Explorations in Performing the Faith*, edited by Wesley Vander Lugt and Trevor Hart, 153–77. Eugene, OR: Cascade, 2014.

Johnson, Todd, and Dale Savidge. *Performing the Sacred: Theology and Theatre in Dialogue*. Engaging Culture. Grand Rapids: Baker, 2009.

Judy Craymer Productions. "Press Centre: Facts and Figures." https://www.judycraymer.com/press-centre/facts-and-figures.php.

Kushner, Robert. "Hiroshi Senju and Makoto Fujimura at Dillon." *Art in America*, December 1995.

Lang, Brent. "Box Office: 'Logan' Slicing and Dicing toward Year's Biggest Debut." *Variety*, March 2, 2017. https://variety.com/2017/film/news/logan-box-office-2017-biggest-debut-1202000089/.

Lendel, Iryna, et al. "Staging Cleveland: A Theater Industry Study." *Urban Publications*, June 2017. https://engagedscholarship.csuohio.edu/urban_facpub/1476/.

Lion King International Tour. "About the International Tour." Michael Cassel Group and Disney Theatrical Productions. http://lionkinginternational.com/about/.

"The Lion King Is Named Most Successful Production of All Time." *BBC News*, September 22, 2014. https://www.bbc.com/news/entertainment-arts-29308447.

MacroTrends. "S&P 500 Historical Annual Returns." https://www.macrotrends.net/2526/sp-500-historical-annual-returns.

Masters, Kim. "'The Hobbit:' Inside Peter Jackson and Warner Bros.' $1 Billion Gamble." *The Hollywood Reporter*, October 17, 2012. https://www.hollywoodreporter.com/news/hobbit-peter-jackson-warner-bros-379301.

McClintock, Pamela. "Box-Office Milestone: 'Black Panther' Joins Billion-Dollar Club." *The Hollywood Reporter*, January 2, 2019. https://www.hollywoodreporter.com/heat-vision/box-office-milestone-black-panther-joins-billion-dollar-club-1093586.

McDonald, Adrian. *2017 Feature Film Study*. Film L.A., August 2018. https://www.filmla.com/wp-content/uploads/2018/08/2017_film_study_v3-WEB.pdf.

McKee, Robert. *Story: Substance, Structure, Style*. New York: Regan, 1997.

McKinley, Jesse. "'Miss Saigon' to End 9-Year Run on Broadway." *New York Times*, April 28, 2000. https://www.nytimes.com/2000/04/28/movies/miss-saigon-to-end-9-year-run-on-broadway.html.

McNary, Dave. "'Finding Dory' Swimming for Record $140 Million Opening." *Variety*, June 18, 2016. https://variety.com/2016/film/news/finding-dory-box-office-record-breaking-opening-weekend-1201798368/.

Bibliography

Mendelson, Scott. "Five Years Ago, 'Avatar' Grossed $2.7 Billion but Left No Pop Culture Footprint." *Forbes*, April 4, 2019. https://www.forbes.com/sites/scottmendelson/2014/12/18/avatar-became-the-highest-grossing-film-of-all-time-while-leaving-no-pop-culture-footprint/.

"Money, Money, Money." *The Economist*, May 3, 2013. https://www.economist.com/graphic-detail/2013/05/03/money-money-money.

Morfoot, Addie. "Producer Says Cats Could Recoup Investment by July." *Crain's New York Business*, December 19, 2016. https://www.crainsnewyork.com/article/20161219/ENTERTAINMENT/161219894/cats-producer-predicts-that-it-will-recoup-by-july.

Ng, David. "'Jersey Boys' Has Been a Windfall for All Involved." *Los Angeles Times*, June 21, 2014. https://www.latimes.com/entertainment/arts/la-et-cm-ca-jersey-boys-musical-20140622-story.html.

Pareti, Tim. "Willow Creek Show Strong at Box Office." *Chicago Tribune*, April 14, 2000. https://www.chicagotribune.com/news/ct-xpm-2000-4-14-004140200-story.html.

Paulson, Michael, and David Gelles. "'Hamilton' Inc.: The Path to a Billion-Dollar Broadway Show." *New York Times*, June 8, 2016. https://www.nytimes.com/2016/06/12/theater/hamilton-inc-the-path-to-a-billion-dollar-show.html.

The Phantom of the Opera. "Facts & Figures." Really Useful Group. https://www.thephantomoftheopera.com/facts-figures/.

Rookmaaker, Hans R. *Art Needs No Justification*. Downers Grove, IL: InterVarsity, 1978.

———. *Modern Art and the Death of Culture*. 2nd ed. 1970. Reprint, Wheaton, IL: Crossway, 2006.

Rubin, Rebecca. "Box Office: 'Aquaman' Debuts at No. 1 with $72 Million, 'Mary Poppins Returns' Beats 'Bumblebee.'" *Reuters*, December 23, 2018. https://www.reuters.com/article/us-usa-boxoffice/box-office-aquaman-debuts-at-no-1-with-72-million-mary-poppins-returns-beats-bumblebee-idUSKCN1OMoI1.

Ryken, Leland. *The Liberated Imagination: Thinking Christianly About the Arts*. Eugene, OR: Wipf and Stock, 2005.

Sakoui, Anousha, and Leslie Patton. "'Incredibles 2' Smashes Record, a Balm for Disney after 'Solo.'" *Bloomberg*, June 16, 2018. https://www.bloomberg.com/news/articles/2018-16-16/-incredibles-2-sets-opening-day-animation-record-for-disney.

Schaeffer, Francis A. *Art and the Bible*. 1973. Reprint, Downers Grove, IL: InterVarsity, 2006.

———. *How Should We Then Live?: The Rise and Decline of Western Thought and Culture*. 1979. Wheaton, IL: Crossway, 2005.

———. *The Roman Age*. Part 1 (disc 1) of *How Should We Then Live?* Directed by John Gosner. Video series on DVD. Originally released on film in 1977. Muskegon, MI: Gospel Films, 2005.

Schaeffer, Frank. *Addicted to Mediocrity*. Wheaton, IL: Crossway, 1981.

Bibliography

Seerveld, Calvin. *Rainbows for the Fallen World: Aesthetic Life and Artistic Task.* Toronto: Tuppence, 1980.

Seymour, Lee. "Over the Last 20 Years, Broadway's 'Lion King' Has Made More Money for Disney than 'Star Wars.'" *Forbes,* December 18, 2017. https://www.forbes.com/sites/leeseymour/2017/12/18/the-lion-king-is-making-more-money-for-disney-than-star-wars/.

Sherbondy, Sharon. "What Happened to Drama in Churches?" *Church Executive,* September 1, 2011. https://churchexecutive.com/archives/what-happened-to-drama-in-churches.

Society of London Theater. "2019 Box Office Figures Released by Society of London Theater." February 25, 2020. https://solt.co.uk/about-london-theatre/press-office/2019-box-office-figures-released-by-society-of-london-theatre/.

Somers, Meredith. "In 'Son of God,' the Bible Told in Low-Budget, Hollywood Style." *Washington Times,* February 27, 2014. http://www.washingtontimes.com/news/2014/feb/27/movie-review-son-of-god/.

Taylor, W. David O., ed. *For the Beauty of the Church: Casting a Vision for the Arts.* Grand Rapids: Baker, 2010.

———. *The Theater of God's Glory: Calvin, Creation, and the Liturgical Arts.* Grand Rapids: Baker, 2017.

Turner, Victor. *From Ritual to Theater: The Human Seriousness of Play.* Baltimore: PAJ, 1982.

Vanhoozer, Kevin J. *The Drama of Doctrine: A Canonical Linguistic Approach to Christian Doctrine.* Louisville: Westminster John Knox, 2005.

———. *Faith Speaking Understanding: Performing the Drama of Doctrine.* Louisville: Westminster John Knox, 2014.

Vander Lugt, Wesley. *Living Theodrama: Reimagining Theological Ethics.* Abingdon, UK: Routledge, 2016.

Vander Lugt, Wesley, and Trevor Hart, eds. *Theatrical Theology: Explorations in Performing the Faith.* Eugene, OR: Cascade, 2014.

Voss, Zannie Giraud, et al. *Theatre Facts 2018: Theatre Communications Group's Report on the Fiscal State of the U.S. Professional Not-for-Profit Theatre Field.* New York: Theatre Communications Group, 2019.

Wax, Kenny. "2019 Box Office Figures Released by Society of London Theatre." Society of London Theatre, February 25, 2020. https://solt.co.uk/about-london-theatre/press-office/2019-box-office-figures-released-by-society-of-london-theatre/.

Wax, Kenny, and Fiona Allan. "2018 Box Office Figures Released by Society of London Theatre and UK Theatre." Society of London Theatre, March 1, 2019. https://solt.co.uk/about-london-theatre/press-office/2018-box-office-figures-released-by-society-of-london-theatre-and-uk-theatre/.

Wells, Samuel. *Improvisation: The Drama of Christian Ethics.* Grand Rapids: Brazos, 2004.

Witchel, Alex. "Is Disney the Newest Broadway Baby?" *New York Times,* April 17, 1994. https://www.nytimes.com/1994/04/17/theater/theater-is-disney-the-newest-broadway-baby.html.

www.ingramcontent.com/pod-product-compliance
Lightning Source LLC
Chambersburg PA
CBHW070927160426
43193CB00011B/1603

"Rakestraw's exploration of the phases of human existence in response to the Creator's purposes and, perhaps most importantly, his treatment of a subject that has become something of an 'elephant in the living room' within contemporary Christianity—the final judgment—is worthy of careful consideration."

—BRUCE PETERSEN
Former Pastor

"Rakestraw has brought his many years of reflecting on biblical and theological truths to provide an informative, thoughtful, helpful, and hopeful look at our journey through this life as humans. . . . This little book will be a meaningful source of spiritual strength for people at all stages of life. I am delighted to recommend this work."

—DAVID S. DOCKERY
Southwestern Baptist Theological Seminary

"I know of no other book like this one: Rakestraw divides humans' lives into seven 'selves,' beginning before birth and continuing to life after death. . . . Rakestraw's evident love for people leads him to urge all to embrace the claims of the true God through Jesus Christ. I loved reading this book, and I know you will too!"

—DAVID M. HOWARD JR.
Bethlehem College and Seminary

"In this book, a mature, conservative Christian theologian views the journey of life through the eyes of faith and infuses his narrative with insights from Scripture and his own reading and rich life experience. The resultant vision is strikingly expansive in scope . . . . The book exudes throughout a confident, faith-based hope regarding what is still to come, and toward which we may dare to lean eagerly forward. Ever moving on."

—GLEN G. SCORGIE
Bethel Seminary

Ever Moving On

Ever Moving On

The Fascinating Journey of Life from the Womb to Beyond the Grave

Robert V. Rakestraw

Foreword by Jane Spriggs

WIPF & STOCK · Eugene, Oregon

EVER MOVING ON

The Fascinating Journey of Life from the Womb to Beyond the Grave

Copyright © 2022 Robert V. Rakestraw. All rights reserved. Except for brief quotations in critical publications or reviews, no part of this book may be reproduced in any manner without prior written permission from the publisher. Write: Permissions, Wipf and Stock Publishers, 199 W. 8th Ave., Suite 3, Eugene, OR 97401.

Wipf & Stock
An Imprint of Wipf and Stock Publishers
199 W. 8th Ave., Suite 3
Eugene, OR 97401

www.wipfandstock.com

PAPERBACK ISBN: 978-1-6667-3458-4
HARDCOVER ISBN: 978-1-6667-9060-3
EBOOK ISBN: 978-1-6667-9061-0

03/22/22

To Judy
With whom I have been moving on for over a half-century, with deepest love, respect, and gratitude beyond the ability of words to express

Contents

Foreword by Jane Spriggs | ix
Preface | xiii

1 The Foundation: The Written and Living Word | 1
2 The First Three Selves | 5
3 The Intermediate Self | 10
4 The Resurrected Self | 21
5 The Judged Self and the Eternal Self: Unbelievers | 31
6 The Judged Self: Believers | 35
7 The Judged Self: Rewards for Believers | 44
8 The Eternal Self: Believers | 56
9 Dangers, Conclusions, and Hope | 68

Appendix: My Credo | 89
Bibliography | 103

Foreword

ROBERT (BOB) RAKESTRAW, THE author of this book, passed away on April 23, 2021. All of us mourn our loss. He was my friend, colleague, mentor—and my pastor. I believe this little book, *Ever Moving On*, may actually be Bob's magnum opus. He wrote it during the final chapter of his life, and we are so grateful to Ashley O'Reilly, his loving and capable granddaughter, for coming alongside him to help bring it to completion. I consider it the pinnacle of Bob's work chiefly because of its subject matter. In it, Bob felt called to address people's two deep questions: What is the meaning of life? and What happens to us after we die? This book moves the readers closer to the answers to these questions—no matter where you find yourself spiritually.

To better understand this book, I'd like you to know a bit about Bob Rakestraw. Bob was a humble man who had a great deal of difficulty talking about himself—but his life and achievements speak for themselves, and others have no difficulty speaking about him.

Bob was in fact a brilliant man. He was an academic who had advanced degrees, including a PhD in theology and religious studies (Drew University, 1985). He was also an accomplished teacher:

Foreword

an instructor in Bible and theology at Prairie Bible Institute, Alberta, Canada, and a theology and ethics professor at Criswell College in Dallas, Texas, and Bethel Seminary in St. Paul, Minnesota. Bob was also an ordained pastor who served churches in Missouri and New Jersey, and he was an author of five books and many professional and popular publications. These are impressive credentials, and Bob took his work seriously.

Bob was a family man. He loved his family: his wife, Judy (who he married fifty-four years ago); his daughters Joni and Laurie; his grandchildren Chloe, Ashley, Katelyn, Tommy, and Jack; and other family members. He didn't take himself too seriously. Ashley's first memory of him was allowing the grandchildren to play doctor and examine Bob's "pregnant" stomach (apparently he'd just eaten)! He always made sure the grandchildren had fun—whether by playing dolls with them, or teaching how to use his treadmill (by the kids sitting on it backwards and then flying into a pillow-filled wall after he turned it on—which delighted Bob a bit more than his wife)!

Bob truly cared about people. He was a professor and mentor to his students; a friend and colleague to faculty and staff, pastors and missionaries; and a person who encouraged people and cared about the lives and spiritual welfare of his family, friends, neighbors, and the people he met. After Bob's death, family members discovered his address book with detailed notes about each person so he could pray for them and ask accurate questions about their lives.

Bob cherished being a child of God. You'll learn more about this from him in *Ever Moving On*. And it wasn't a secret to his family that Bob loved God.

Bob's grandchildren often visited him in his office, where he explained his writing projects to them, told them that Jesus loved them, and challenged them to read the Bible (even providing financial rewards if they read a chapter in the Bible for thirty-one days—one granddaughter read the biblical book Genesis).

And Bob demonstrated by his life what a follower of Jesus looked like. He was a grateful man, even though he experienced

Foreword

great physical suffering for more than thirty years. Bob's positive life experiences as well as his struggles with heart disease, a heart transplant, and subsequent rejection of his new heart are detailed in his autobiographical book *GraceQuest*.

Even though he had a chronic illness that restricted his life and work for many years, our friend Bob did not become a bitter or angry man. He wasn't afraid to die, and acknowledged that he was alive because God still had work for him to do on earth. This work included his writing, praying for many people, and sharing his wisdom with friends and colleagues as they visited Bob in his Minnesota or Arizona homes.

Bob often stated that he knew God was with him, even in the midst of his suffering. One poignant example of this is when, after his heart transplant, Bob told his sister Rosemary and her family how he had sensed Jesus standing in the doorway of his bedroom, loving him, and walking over to give him a hug. It was a profound moment that Bob, and his family, never forgot.

This book includes quite a bit of material about life after death, but it isn't depressing. In fact, it is hopeful, and that's the way Bob felt about the end of his life. He longed for heaven and couldn't wait to begin, as he says, the longest part of his life—the part that takes place after our deaths.

I encourage you to read *Ever Moving On* and meditate the Bible verses he has chosen to explain his positions on life, death, and life after death. Allow God to speak to you about faith in Jesus. To repeat some of the words Bob chose as his final plea to you, his readers, from C. S. Lewis' book, *Mere Christianity*:

> Give up yourself, and you will find your real self. Lose your life and you will save it. Submit to death, death of your ambitions and favorite wishes every day and death of your whole body in the end: submit with every fiber of your being, and you will find eternal life . . . look for Christ, and you will find Him, and with Him, everything else thrown in.

Foreword

This book will lead you closer to God and the life he has for you today on earth, and in eternity.

Jane Spriggs, MDiv
Pastor, Evangelical Covenant Church
Coauthor, with Bob Rakestraw, of
Heart Cries: Praying by the Spirit in the Midst of Life
October 29, 2021

Preface

IT MAY WELL BE that the two deepest questions people have asked since the beginning of civilization are: What is the meaning of life? and What happens to us after we die? In our more recent, postmodern world, however, these questions seem to have been eclipsed considerably by such questions as: How can I find happiness? and Does anybody really love me for who I am?

While the latter questions may be more prevalent today, especially in the minds of younger people, the former ones retain or regain their prominence as the years of life pass by, as we move on to our more mature selves. This little book will address the first two questions primarily, although answers to the other questions are surely wrapped within the more foundational issues, and will receive attention as well.

Welcome to the incredible journey of the seven selves. In the following pages we will consider together the adventure of life from our earliest hours in our mother's womb to our life beyond the grave.

This is a path all of us are traveling, and everyone benefits by thinking about where we are on the highway and how we are managing to move along. I have personally experienced remarkable

Preface

benefits by thinking deliberately of my journey, and I long to share some thoughts on these matters with my fellow travelers.

This book is titled *Ever Moving On*, since our lives may be characterized, as much as anything, by movement. Even when we are loafing or sleeping, we are moving forward through the days. No matter what, time passes and we age, one day after the other. From early childhood our most common form of movement is walking. We travel through life, often literally, by putting one foot in front of the other. Visualizing the activity of walking, as well as doing it, will be helpful in moving through our interesting yet difficult existence.

The most popular religious book of all time, except for the Bible, is *The Pilgrim's Progress*, a story about moving on—about walking through life. It was written by John Bunyan and first published in England in 1678. This small classic has been translated into over two hundred languages, and remains a bestseller for adults and children alike. Charles Spurgeon, sometimes described as "the prince of preachers," read the book one hundred times.

The author, who left school at the age of ten, wrote this allegory of a pilgrim—his name was Christian—while he (Bunyan) was in the Bedfordshire county prison, where he was held intermittently for twelve-and-a-half years as a political prisoner for his nonconformist religious views and activities.

The title page of the first printing reads: *The Pilgrim's Progress from This World, to That Which Is to Come, Delivered Under the Similitude of a Dream*. Writing in the first person, Bunyan relates his "dream" (a literary device) of the pilgrim's journey through life from the City of the World to the Celestial City (the Holy City, the New Jerusalem).[1]

From Christian's early years as a searcher after truth he walks the rough, dangerous, and confusing highway of life, facing numerous obstacles and severe trials. He encounters many individuals

---

1. It is no wonder that *The Pilgrim's Progress* has been published, and continues to be, in a wide variety of printings, bindings, illustrative patterns, and prices. Many editions are easily available online and in libraries.

Preface

along the way, some helpful (such as Evangelist and Hope) and some adversarial (such as Obstinate and Giant Despair).

Christian's strengths and weaknesses are presented in simple yet profound language that resonates with all who pursue truth, lasting relief from the burdens of life, and a purpose for living. Perhaps in some respects we may be helped by thinking of this pilgrim "moving on" as we consider our own progress from the womb to life beyond the grave.

In the very early church, as soon as people were believing in Jesus and persuading others to do the same, the first Christians—because of their beliefs and lifestyle—became known as followers of "the Way." The book of Acts records a number of instances using this early descriptive term for Christianity.

The first of these references states that "Saul was still breathing out murderous threats against the Lord's disciples. He went to the high priest and asked him for letters to the synagogues in Damascus, so that if he found any there who belonged to the Way, whether men or women, he might take them as prisoners to Jerusalem" (Acts 9:1-2).

After Saul was converted, and began to be called Paul, the text states that Paul spoke boldly in the synagogue at Ephesus for three months, "arguing persuasively about the kingdom of God. But some of them became obstinate; they refused to believe and publicly maligned the Way" (Acts 19:8-9).

After over two years of Paul's teaching and evangelistic ministry in Ephesus, "there arose a great disturbance about the Way" (Acts 19:23), leading to a riot over the implications of the gospel of Christ. (See more about "the Way" in Acts 16:17; 18:25-26; 22:4; 24:14, 22; and 2 Pet 2:2). Jesus designated himself as "the way" (John 14:6), and those who follow the Jesus way faithfully, as did John Bunyan's Christian, will experience both opposition and encouragement often.

In this little volume I do not intend to present some clever words and artificial solutions to the issues of life, as though I have all the answers to your questions. However, I do intend that this book will lead you significantly closer to the answers you are

Preface

searching for, and the life of joy, purpose, and fulfillment you long for. This intention applies whether you are a nonbeliever or a believer in God, an agnostic or a skeptic, spiritual but not religious, or one who is totally convinced of the reality and activity of God in the world: past, present, and future.

I am one of those "totally convinced." I have served as a pastor of churches in Missouri and New Jersey, but most of my life I have taught biblical studies, theology, ethics, and preaching at the undergraduate and graduate levels of three colleges and seminaries. My most recent service, before taking early retirement due to health concerns related to the rejection of my transplanted heart, was as professor of theology at Bethel Seminary in St. Paul, Minnesota, where I taught for seventeen years (1988–2005). I have been married to Judy since 1967, and we have two children and five grandchildren. My life story is entitled *GraceQuest: One Teacher's Relentless Pursuit of Salvation, Spirituality, and the Grace to Suffer Well*.[2]

I am deeply concerned about the physical, psychological, and spiritual welfare of everyone I know, and of everyone I don't know, because I believe strongly that God is also deeply concerned for every child, woman, and man on our planet.

This is a book about the seven sequential "selves" of human existence, from conception to eternity future. The first two of these, which I will explain shortly, may be considered by human reason alone. No special revelation (guidance from God) is needed to think about these selves. The other five, however, require revelation to understand, because they are far beyond our human intelligence and wisdom to comprehend. To this matter we turn next.

---

2. Information on this book and other writings by Dr. Rakestraw is available at gracequestministries.org.

1

The Foundation
The Written and Living Word

THE REVELATION TO WHICH I refer is the Bible, a truly remarkable work that is deservedly the bestselling book of all time. It was written by about forty individuals, each working alone or mostly alone (although some knew one another), led by God over a period of about 1,600 years, throughout the Middle East and southeastern Europe primarily. Along with billions of God's people who have gone before, as well as hundreds of millions now living, I affirm without hesitation that these biblical writings—the Hebrew-Christian scriptures—are the written word of God.

Such a view of the Bible does not claim that it was all dictated by God. With most of the Bible, God led the human authors to write in an inspired and trustworthy manner—using their own vocabularies, writing styles, and personalities, within the thought-forms and cultures of their day—concerning the activities of the Lord and his people in bringing redemption and blessing to the world.

Everything in the Bible, including the good and evil deeds of humans, angels, and devils, has been recorded under the sovereign direction of God for our temporal and eternal benefit. The Bible makes these astonishing claims for itself (2 Tim 3:14–17; 2 Pet

1:12–21; Rom 15:4; see also Ps 119:11–20, 71–77), and this fact in itself ought to prompt everyone to investigate such claims.

Why, you might ask, do I have such a high view of an admittedly human-authored book? How can I speak of the Bible as "the written word of God," and consider it the only infallible, only divinely authoritative written revelation for people everywhere: the supreme and essential guidebook for all of life—this life and the life to come?

There are numerous, substantial reasons for my conviction, ones that many wise thinkers have offered over the centuries. Here are just two, presented very briefly.

The first consideration is the striking pattern of biblical prophecies and their precise fulfillments, in some cases hundreds of years later. Two examples (out of many) of this pattern are: (1) the highly accurate prediction of the multi-phased destruction of the wicked city of Tyre in Ezek 26, and its exact fulfillment under Nebuchadnezzar and Alexander the Great over the next few centuries, confirmed by careful historical research and archaeology; and (2) the naming of Bethlehem as the birthplace of the Messiah, Jesus of Nazareth, in Mic 5:2, centuries before the first Christmas. Such precise historical realities would have been impossible to predict in the natural realm, and were obviously directed by the only all-knowing and all-powerful Lord of all.

A second argument is based on the life of Jesus Christ, the remarkable man of God who lived in the first century AD. His teachings, his miracles, his fulfilled prophecies, his resurrection from the dead, and his authoritative yet compassionate message and manner while ministering to the people of his day, constitute the most convincing line of reasoning to me (and a large number of others) for the divine authorship of the Bible.

By this I refer to the reality that this man Jesus—in my opinion the wisest, most holy, most truthful, most down-to-earth human being in the history of civilization—(1) emphatically and repeatedly endorsed the scriptures of his day (now called the Old Testament) as the infallible and authoritative word of God; and (2) declared that the Holy Spirit of God would come after him to

The Foundation: The Written and Living Word

reveal to his disciples the further truth they would need to carry on the work he began during his earthly life (now called the New Testament, revealed to be applied over the following two thousand years and more by the Spirit's teaching).

Since this most remarkable human being gave such forceful witness to the inspiration, truthfulness, and godly authority of the Bible, the written word (communication) of God, and spoke of himself plainly as the living word (communication) of God, I gladly and confidently place my trust in the Bible.

Some may reply, however, that the above is a "circular argument"—using the Bible to prove the Bible. The above way of reasoning would indeed be an unacceptable logical fallacy if we begin with the assumption that the Bible is divinely revealed. But we are not doing such. Instead, we begin with the far less controversial realization that the biblical documents—in this case the Gospel accounts—are worthy to be read and acknowledged simply as valuable ancient writings from four competent authors who present the story, from four different perspectives, of a highly unusual person.[1]

This striking individual has been considered by multitudes over the centuries to be the most pivotal figure in human history. (Our calendar, for example, is divided into BC [Latin, "before Christ"] and AD [Latin, *Anno Domini*, "in the year of the Lord"].) Such a fascinating person deserves to be studied and analyzed extensively and intensively, from all angles, as he has been. Any documents written close to the lifetime of Jesus, as the Gospels were, must be considered especially valuable historically.

The Gospels (Matthew, Mark, Luke, and John) are four well-researched and well-written historical/theological accounts placed at the start of the New Testament that present the life, teachings, and works of Jesus. Even if some people are unwilling to accept the divine inspiration of the Gospels, yet consider them as valuable ancient writings from the first century, such thinkers may still study these Gospels with an open mind, and conclude—even as a good many non-Christians have—that they are indeed accurate

---

1. Some wise insights concerning the circularity objection are in Carson, *Collected Writings on Scripture*, 35–37.

accounts of the life of Jesus. From that conclusion they may then come to believe—as many skeptics have after careful study and reflection (especially reading the Gospels themselves with an open mind)—that Jesus is indeed the *living* Word of God and the scriptures are indeed the *written* Word of God.

This line of reasoning, admittedly quite brief, explains my conviction that the Bible, authenticated by Jesus, is the only reliable written foundation for the following journey of the seven selves. Without it I would be simply spinning ideas and speculations out of my very limited and fallible mind, with nothing but possibility and perhaps some probability, along with some wishful thinking, to try to guide those who read this.[2] In the following pages I will quote much from the Bible, and refer to it heavily even when I do not quote it, because I am convinced without doubt that the scriptures are the inspired truth of God Almighty himself.[3]

---

2. A good place to begin studying, at a non-specialist's level, the historical evidence for the reliability of the gospels and the integrity of Jesus is Strobel, *Case for Christ*. Valuable works discussing the evidence for the Bible's inspiration, as well as the principal objections to belief in Christ are Strobel, *Case for Faith*; Helm, "Faith, Evidence, and the Scriptures"; and Wenham, *Christ and the Bible*.

3. All quotations from and references to the Bible, unless indicated otherwise, are from the New International Version (2011 text). For additional explanatory notes, charts, cross-references, essays, outlines, and a partial concordance, I highly recommend either *NIV Study Bible* or *NIV Biblical Theology Study Bible* (previously published as *NIV Zondervan Study Bible*). With each of these hefty Bibles having over 2,500 pages, you will need a sturdy desk or table, or a solid lap and strong wrists, to work with these excellent tools. In addition, many have found the also-hefty and also-valuable *Life Application Study Bible* to be a useful guide in the practical aspects of daily life and service. It is available in several translations, including the well-regarded New Living Translation. I consider a good study Bible to be the most valuable thing a person can possess.

2

The First Three Selves

WHAT PROMPTED ME TO write this book—one that started simply as a brief essay for my website—was the death of my mother-in-law during the year 2019. Blanche Engevik was a delightful, loving, and unselfish woman of God who went to be with her Lord in glory at the age of 95. A much-loved mother of eight, Blanche was wonderfully wise and steady, and her celebratory memorial service affected all who attended. Her homegoing led me to think about the major transition points and phases of existence during a person's lifetime, from conception to eternity future.

Each of the transition points can be thought of as the beginning of a new "self," a word that Webster's dictionary defines (for our purposes here) as "the identity, character, or essential qualities of any person." While we live all of our years as one continuing "self" (oneself), it is possible and, I trust, helpful to everyone reading this, to differentiate a number of sequential "selves" as we move through this life and beyond. (The sections of this book are of uneven length because I desire to devote most attention to the relatively unknown topic of life after death, especially for the believer.)

First, there is the Initial Self, begun at conception. When the sperm and egg from our parents united, we began to exist. Within that fertilized egg (except in certain cases of genetic abnormality) were contained all things essential for our development as human beings, as long as we were attached to our mother and protected in her womb (Ps 139:13–16).

Second, there is the Independent Self, begun at birth. When our little body was separated from that of our mother we began to live in a completely different matrix: air, along with fabric, human touch from outside, and all manner of things. During our early years in this new mode of existence we were totally dependent on others for our survival and nurture, yet in one relatively brief moment of time, at our birth, we became materially (as a body) an unattached and independent self. The Bible refers to this self as the old self, in contrast to the new self (Eph 4:22–24; Col 3:9–10).

Third, there is the In-Christ Self, begun at regeneration. This is the moment when God regenerates a person: gives new life—spiritual life—to that individual. We may think of this as another conception, a spiritual one. The divine seed or sperm—God's very life—enters and unites with the human "egg" (the human being) and regenerates (but does not obliterate) the person (the Independent Self) and makes a new creation.

This is the moment of new birth, which Jesus spoke of as being born again (John 3:3–8; see also 1:9–13). This is the beginning of the new self. The Apostle Paul declared that "if anyone is in Christ, the new creation has come: The old has gone, the new is here" (2 Cor 5:17; see also 1 Cor 15:22). "He saved us through the washing of rebirth ("regeneration" in the King James Version) and renewal by the Holy Spirit" (Titus 3:5).

One of the most important designations for believers in the New Testament writings is those who are "in Christ." This is the magnificent, historic doctrine of a believer's union with Christ, from which flows all other dynamics pertaining to the believer's life here on earth and throughout eternity (John 15:1–4; 17:26; Gal 2:20; Eph 1:1–4; 4:32; Phil 1:1; 2:1–2).

This transaction is that of which Peter writes: "For you have been born again, not of perishable seed, but of imperishable, through the living and enduring word of God (1 Pet 1:13). (It is

The First Three Selves

interesting to realize that the Greek word here for "seed" is *spora*, from which we get "spore," and the Greek word for "seed" in 1 John 3:9, which speaks of "God's seed" living in those who are "born of God," is *sperma*, from which we get our word "sperm.")

While we had nothing to do initially with becoming our first two selves, we are invited and commanded to enter into this third self, our new life in Christ, as taught in the above-mentioned texts from the Gospel of John and in such passages as Acts 2:37–41; 3:19–20; and 2 Cor 5:17—6:2. Even though God is the One who works this change in us, so that our salvation is not accomplished by any effort of our own or of anyone else (John 1:12–13; Eph 2:8–9), we are expected and enabled by our loving Father to receive this gift of new life by our personal choice, through repentance and faith in Jesus Christ.

Does Baptism Bring About a New Self?

Some churches teach that the new birth is accomplished through baptism. This is such a widely held view within Christianity that it deserves attention here, especially as it relates to infants.

Many (though not all) of those who baptize babies teach that the divine work of rebirth takes place by means of this ceremony. Such clergy may affirm that God, not the water, does the regenerating work in the one being baptized, but the impression is sometimes conveyed quite strongly that the baptismal ceremony (rite, sacrament) is essential to, and causative in, the new birth for eternal life.

The scriptures clearly teach, however, that baptism is to *follow* one's conscious personal decision to receive Christ, and that baptism is a public testimony of one's prior reception of Christ through faith, even if such a decision is made shortly before baptism. A baby cannot make a choice to believe in Christ, nor can anyone do that for them. The scriptures also teach emphatically that one's salvation through the new birth is a gift of God, not of works or any human action.

Confusion in the minds of some Christians may be due to the fact that, in the early years of the Christian church, the "conversion" event involved three elements that were understood as being practically inseparable: belief in Jesus Christ as Savior and Lord, baptism in (or by, or with) the Holy Spirit, and water baptism.

Concerning Spirit baptism, this is best understood as the Father's work (gift) of immersing every newborn believer into one "spiritual water, "—the very Holy Spirit—so that all who are "in" this ocean of divine love, power, and holiness are one spiritual body in Christ, his universal church (Luke 24:45–49; Acts 1:4–5; 2:32–41; 9:17–19; 10:43–48; 11:15–18; and especially 1 Cor 12:13).

While the newly developing church needed time—as led by God—to fully integrate new believers from four different backgrounds (Jews, half-Jews [Samaritans], non-Jews [Gentiles], and the disciples of John the Baptist) into the one universal body of Christ (as seen throughout the book of Acts), the order that emerges (theologically) in the conversion event is, as stated above, faith in Jesus, Spirit baptism, and water baptism. The first two of these occur at the same time, even though some (erroneously, I believe) teach that Spirit baptism—demonstrated by speaking in tongues—must be pursued and attained by every Christian after they receive Christ, unless they spoke in tongues at the time of their conversion.

Concerning water baptism, in the New Testament church, after the divinely led development of Christian experience and teaching on these matters over a period of some twenty-five years (recorded in Acts 1:1—19:10), there was no such category as "unbaptized Christian." From the beginning, our Lord intended belief to be followed by baptism in water (Matt 28:18–20). (The Greek word *baptizo*, the verb behind our noun "baptism," means to dip or immerse, even plunge, drench, or overwhelm.)

Water baptism was (and is) to be the outward sign of the inward change in us (regeneration accompanied by Spirit baptism), as our testimony to the world that our old life (old self) was crucified with Christ and that we are now new selves in him (Rom 6:1–14; Gal 2:20; 6:14–15). When a person comes forward to be baptized,

The First Three Selves

they are choosing to identify publicly with the followers of Jesus Christ and acknowledging openly that he is their Savior and Lord, and they are renouncing all other higher or competing allegiances.

However we think about infant baptism, believer's baptism, and Spirit baptism, our confidence for our new birth, our new self, and our new way of life must be in God alone, never in anything done to us or for us by human beings, in ceremonies, or through formulas, and not even in our prayer to receive Christ, as though it was our accomplishment or meritorious work.

Those ministers who choose to baptize babies, for what they believe are valid reasons, must be clear (even as those who baptize older children and adults need to be clear) during the ceremonies and during the times of instruction with the parents and candidates, that there is no saving power in the rite of baptism. As important as it is to follow Jesus by receiving water baptism, and as surely as it is a means of grace whereby God blesses and strengthens us, it has no power in itself to bring about the new birth required by Jesus and the New Testament scriptures.[1]

Those who enter into the third-self category, the In-Christ Self, enter by their God-empowered volition. This is not something that happens to a person automatically, as in the cases of the Initial Self and the Independent Self. It is a terrible mistake—a very serious, even fatal, error—to assume that people who grow up in a "Christian" culture will gradually become "in Christ" apart from the saving work of God in them, received normatively through their intentional repentance and faith, leading to eternal life (John 6:35-44, 63-65).[2]

---

1. A valuable book, written jointly by a proponent of infant baptism and a proponent of baptism for believers only, is Bridge and Phypers, *Water That Divides*. In addition, Hallesby, *Infant Baptism*, thoughtfully presents the case for infant baptism, while Jeschke, *Believers Baptism for Children*, offers a rather different approach for supporters of believer baptism by arguing against both traditional infant baptism *and* the direct imposition of the New Testament model (conversion followed by soon baptism of adults) upon children who grow up in the church.

2. Those wishing to pursue further the matter of a necessary, personal commitment to Jesus Christ will be helped considerably by Lewis, *Mere Christianity*; Hallesby, *Why I Am a Christian;* and Laidlaw, *Reasons Why*.

3

The Intermediate Self

As indicated above, the self is the identity, character, essential qualities, and total being of a person. The self is who one is at their core, first of all materially (bodily) but also, as time passes, who one is as a developed human being: body, mind, will, emotions, relatability, likes and dislikes, personality, and spirituality.

In contrast to the first two selves (the Initial Self and the Independent Self) into which we entered involuntarily, the third self (the In-Christ Self) can only be begun in us by an act of our will—a choice to receive Jesus Christ as Lord and Savior for our earthly life and all eternity. Jesus spoke of this radical change as a "crossing over" in John 5:24: "Very truly I tell you, whoever hears my word and believes him who sent me has eternal life and will not be judged but has crossed over from death to life."

With regard to these first two or three selves, we are now who we are, *having been and continuing to be* in each previous phase of our one (unified) ongoing self (oneself). You will always be you, and I will always be me, as products of our previous selves. In a sense, we "recapitulate" (swallow up and retain) all that we have been previously, from our conception in our mother's womb and

The Intermediate Self

over the years to the present. There is a continuity to our personal identity beneath all these transitions and changes.

The person who has not been born again by the Spirit of God is the Independent Self "in Adam," while the regenerated person (still "in Adam" in some respects, e.g., we will all die) is now a new self: the In-Christ Self (John 3:1–21; 1 Cor 1:30; 15:21–22; 2 Cor 5:17; Eph 4:22–24; Col 3:9–10; Titus 3:5). The old self is said by Jesus to be living right now in spiritual death, as seen in John 5:24, quoted above.

The fourth self, the Intermediate Self, begins at bodily death. Whether a person has lived through all three of the previous selves or only the first two, that individual will enter this intermediate realm at the moment of his or her death. This is the mysterious land of the dead, which popular authors and filmmakers never cease to present imaginatively to a public that craves knowledge of what lies on the other side, and whether those who go there communicate with or even return to those on this side.

Whenever we attend a funeral or memorial service, we know, if we are Bible-believing Christians, that the one being remembered is alive spiritually in a state of either comfort or agony (Luke 16:25), as determined by their previous choices. For this reason, some funerals we attend are very difficult for us to sit through.

While we live on earth, except when God may sovereignly intervene, we exercise our will—our power of choosing—freely and continually. We decide to shop at this store rather than that one. We choose to associate with this person rather than that one. We decide to live with God or without him. When we die, however (and from God's perspective, even before), our ability to choose for or against God comes to an end. This is clearly the idea behind the solemn words of the angel to John, in the last chapter of the Bible:

> Do not seal up the words of the prophecy of this scroll, because the time is near. Let the one who does wrong continue to do wrong; let the vile person continue to be vile; let the one who does right continue to do right; and let the holy person continue to be holy. (Rev 22:10–11)

The angel, speaking for God, is referring to the fact that both the redeemed and the lost in view here, still living their lives on earth, have made their choice for or against God, and God knows they are confirmed in that choice. They will not change, so let them be, following the desires of their hearts. Their eternal destiny has been determined by their decisions and actions throughout their lives. These words of the angel are sobering indeed.

Life After Death: What Is It?

What precisely is the Intermediate Self, and what is the intermediate state—that realm or place in which intermediate selves exist? If everyone, believer and nonbeliever, enters this new phase of conscious selfhood at death, as I believe the Bible teaches, what is that life like? One interesting question, among others, concerns whether everyone receives some kind of intermediate body at that time. That there will someday be a resurrection of both the saved and the lost is taught plainly in Dan 12:2–3 and John 5:24–29. But what is the present material state, if there is one, of those who have passed on and who are now awaiting the ultimate resurrection spoken of by Daniel and John?

The answer to this question has been debated for centuries, and has generated considerable speculation, since the Bible does not answer the question directly. Some even debate whether there is an intermediate state at all, at least one in which individuals are conscious.

∼

Many have argued that when a person dies they either (1) go immediately into their eternal state with their new resurrection body received at the time of death; or (2) continue to exist in a state of soul sleep, without a body or consciousness, until the resurrection; or (3) become extinct (body and soul) at death—both believers and nonbelievers—and then are recreated by God at the end of time, during the events associated with the return of Christ; or (4) are

The Intermediate Self

annihilated by God, after their judgment, if they are nonbelievers; or (5) enter a place for believers only, called purgatory, where their souls are purified and disciplined in proportion to their earthly sins until God takes them finally to heaven.

Because each of the above theories is without serious biblical support, we will not consider them here, except to note that the first view above has a bit more plausibility than the others, and some Christian theologians express openness to it. These say (accurately I believe) that *if* the redeemed who die now enter the final (eternal) state at the moment of death (perhaps just after appearing before a private judgment seat of Christ spoken of in 2 Cor 5:8–10) with their resurrection bodies given to them at that time, such a transaction must be viewed from a non-earthly perspective of time, one of which we can have no present knowledge. Even so, 1 Thess 4:16 ("the dead in Christ shall rise first" at Christ's coming) presents a serious difficulty for this view, since the dead in Christ would already have their resurrection bodies.

Time and Eternity

With regard to the issue of time in eternity, theologian Stanley Grenz, in *Theology for the Community of God*, contributes some intriguing insights and speculations in the following quotations:

> Crucial to any helpful conception of the intermediate state is our understanding of time and eternity. We cannot grasp fully how time is present to eternity.... [Death] marks the boundary not only of earthly life, but consequently between the earthly and the eternal experiences of time.... [The dead person] senses no gap between death and the eschatological resurrection.
>
> This does not mean that the dead immediately experience the resurrection, however. Being uninvolved in earthly events does not mean that they are completely disconnected from these occurrences. On the contrary, while not active agents in earthly events, in a special sense the dead are aware of what is happening on earth.

Ever Moving On

> Yet we must understand this cognition by appeal to their changed perspective toward time.
>
> We experience events as travelers through time from the present and into the future and therefore as disconnected units *en route* to the end. In eternity, however, we will know earthly time as the unified whole which from God's perspective it actually is. Seen from the perspective beyond earthly time, the dead share God's composite perspective. They are not conscious of earthly events as isolated occurrences but as integrated into a whole.
>
> A specific situation may serve to illustrate this concept. We often inquire as to whether a deceased loved one might be aware of our grieving in the face of his or her death. This person is aware, we assert. But he or she is not cognizant of our grief in the manner that characterizes earthly awareness, namely, as an isolated event in the process of time. Rather, our loved one knows our grief in the context of the whole of time, specifically as it is eschatologically overcome in the joy of our reunion in the resurrection.[1]

For those interested in thinking further on these fascinating issues, the late Stanley Grenz—now himself in the intermediate state of which he wrote—has additional insights and speculations in his book, as does theologian Millard Erickson in his *Christian Theology*.[2] Many others have written on this intriguing topic.

The best view of these matters, according to my (obviously imperfect) understanding, is that at death everyone enters a phase that we may refer to as the Intermediate Self. Such a deceased individual is a conscious self, either comforted or suffering, awaiting their resurrection. The question lingers, however: does such a person exist, temporarily, in an embodied or a disembodied state? Some Bible-believing theologians prefer the view that such selves are disembodied: they exist as fully aware souls, personal

---

1. Grenz, *Theology*, 97–98.
2. Erickson, *Christian Theology*, 1179–90.

communicative entities, yet without corporeal substance. Others see them as somehow embodied.

Concerning bodily selfhood after death for those in this state, especially unbelievers, the central scripture passage is Luke 16:19–31. This is a truly terrifying account, narrated by Jesus, of a rich man and a beggar named Lazarus existing in the afterlife. The rich man is in terrible suffering, while the beggar is comforted. There is a debate about whether the words of Jesus here are an imaginative parable or a factual description, but in either case the account was clearly intended to teach some startling truths about this life and the afterlife, for both believers and unbelievers. The language of Jesus indicates that the individuals involved had material bodies (vss 23–24).

Beyond the question of embodiment, however, we do well to keep in mind that in no other parable does Jesus mention specific names. It seems best—because most natural—to read the story in Luke 16 as a true account, known perfectly to the God who sees and knows all. Jesus presents this narrative in relation to earthly time, but the shocking realities disclosed carry over into eternity.

Bible Verses about Deceased Believers

It will be helpful and edifying at this point to present some pertinent scriptures relating to *believers* in the intermediate state. With some of these scriptures we cannot say with certainty that they pertain to our existence immediately after death rather than later, but they may. In any case, they reveal God's heart of love to his children after he calls them home. And this is the most important thing.

Also, while the following texts do not tell us about our bodily condition after death, they bring us some direct word from God's Word to guide our thoughts and hearts to what matters most about the intermediate state. (It is important to note that sleep in the Bible, when referring to the deceased, does not indicate a lack of consciousness, but refers to the way we on earth contemplate their dead bodies and think of them as resting from the affairs of this life.)

Ever Moving On

Therefore my heart is glad and my tongue rejoices; my body also will rest secure, because you will not abandon me to the realm of the dead, nor will you let your faithful one see decay. You make known to me the path of life; you will fill me with joy in your presence, with eternal pleasures at your right hand. (Ps 16:9–11)

But God will redeem me from the realm of the dead; he will surely take me to himself. (Ps 49:15)

Yet I am always with you; you hold me by my right hand. You guide me with your counsel, and afterward you will take me into glory. (Ps 73:23–24)

Truly I tell you, some who are standing here will not taste death before they see the kingdom of God. About eight days after Jesus said this, he took Peter, John, and James with him and went up onto a mountain to pray. As he was praying, the appearance of his face changed, and his clothes became as bright as a flash of lightning. Two men, Moses and Elijah, appeared in glorious splendor, talking with Jesus. They spoke about his departure, which he was about to bring to fulfillment at Jerusalem. (Luke 9:27–31)

But Abraham replied, "Son, remember that in your lifetime you received your good things, while Lazarus received bad things, but now he is comforted here and you are in agony. And besides all this, between us and you a great chasm has been set in place, so that those who want to go from here to you cannot, nor can anyone cross over from there to us." (Luke 16:25–26)

Then he [the repentant criminal at Calvary] said, "Jesus, remember me when you come into your kingdom." Jesus answered him, "Truly I tell you, today you will be with me in paradise." (Luke 23:42–43)

While they were stoning him, Stephen prayed, "Lord Jesus, receive my spirit." Then he fell on his knees and cried out, "Lord, do not hold this sin against them." When he had said this, he fell asleep. (Acts 7:59–60)

The Intermediate Self

> For we know that if the earthly tent we live in is destroyed, we have a building from God, an eternal house in heaven, not built by human hands. Meanwhile we groan, longing to be clothed instead with our heavenly dwelling, because when we are clothed, we will not be found naked. . . . Therefore, we are always confident and know that as long as we are at home in the body we are away from the Lord. For we live by faith, not by sight. We are confident, I say, and would prefer to be away from the body and at home with the Lord. (2 Cor 5:1–3, 6–8)

> For to me, to live is Christ and to die is gain. . . . I desire to depart and be with Christ, which is better by far. . . . (Phil 1:21, 23)

> Brothers and sisters, we do not want you to be uninformed about those who sleep in death, so that you do not grieve like the rest of mankind, who have no hope. For . . . the dead in Christ will rise first. After that, we who are still alive and are left will be caught up together with them in the clouds to meet the Lord in the air. And so we will be with the Lord forever. Therefore encourage one another with these words. (1 Thess 4:13, 16–18)

These scriptures are so uplifting (even though perplexing in parts) to all of God's people that it seems rather unimportant—even trivial and unwise, according to some—to ask whether believers between death and resurrection exist as embodied or disembodied spirits. The fact is that we simply cannot know, although it does seem strange (yet not impossible[3]) that anyone would be able to exist personally without some kind of body.

We can know, however, that deceased believers, including our friends and loved ones, are right now personal selves in God's actual presence. They are communicating with him and are very much alive, comforted, and blessed abundantly. I believe that they may even be dancing together with levels of energy and delight beyond anything that we can possibly imagine.

---

3. Erickson, *Christian Theology*, 1189.

Will We Know Our Loved Ones in the Intermediate State?

Can believers in the intermediate state communicate with one another, and will we know our loved ones in that wonderful realm of life? I believe that they do communicate, and that we will know one another. I must admit, though, that there is not a lot in the Bible to support this twofold assumption directly, even though for me it is enough. Several lines of thought lead me to this conclusion.

The biblical texts just quoted emphasize, above all, the comfort and joy we will experience in the presence and company of God. This is as it should be, since our greatest delight will be in seeing and speaking with God himself. However, we may reasonably question whether we will exist as isolated individuals with our own separate access to God, but without the ability to recognize or speak with one another, including friends and family we knew well on earth. After all, there is so much emphasis in the Bible on fellowship and strong relationships with other believers in *this* life (Mal 3:16–18; John 19:26–27; Acts 2:46–47; Rom 16:1–16; 1 Thess 2:17–20; Heb 10:23–25).

We should also keep in mind that our Lord is presently working on the greatest construction project of all time, our heavenly dwellings (John 14:1–3; Heb 11:13–16, 39–40; see also John 17:24). Is he building "mansions" or apartment units where the saved live only in isolation, or only in relationships with totally new acquaintances, but not long-time friends and relatives from earth? To me, the answers to these questions seem obvious.

Furthermore, the earlier-cited passage in Luke 9 records the occasion when Peter, John, and James were with Jesus on the mountain. The appearance of Jesus changed dramatically, and the disciples saw and heard Moses and Elijah, in glorious splendor, speaking with Jesus about the events soon to happen, evidently concerning his death and resurrection. Here we have the amazing revelation that Moses and Elijah, still in their intermediate state, return to earth to talk theology with Jesus, undoubtedly as a learning experience for the disciples and for us as we get a peek into the world beyond this one.

The two Old Testament servants of God appear to be alive and well, obviously knowing each other (even though their earthly lifetimes did not overlap) and interacting with each other and Jesus as they all spoke together—discussing theology. While this was a very special occurrence, it gives us important insight into the realm awaiting us. This is recorded in God's word for our benefit, probably intended in more than one way.

There are other scriptures that can stimulate our thinking about the possibility of personal interaction in the intermediate state, even though they may pertain as much or more to our final state (1 Thess 4:13-18; Rev 7:9-17). One text, however, in Rev 6:9-11, speaks of a robing ceremony in the intermediate state, where under the altar "the souls of those who had been slain because of the word of God and the testimony they had maintained" pray together in a loud voice, after which each receives a white robe and listens to some instructions to "wait a little longer." From reading this passage I get the impression that these martyrs had some communication with one another as intermediate selves, and previously knew one another on earth—at least some of them. They also seemed to know what was happening on earth.

While we ought not to construct, from the texts just mentioned, a fully developed theology of interpersonal knowledge and communication in the intermediate state, we likewise ought not to ignore these scriptures in thinking about matters that concern us deeply here on earth regarding our friends and loved ones—and ourselves one day—in the intermediate state.

Final Words

Unfortunately, as we conclude our brief reflections on the intermediate state, we must again mention, if only briefly, the experience of unbelievers between their death and the resurrection presently awaiting them. Just as we cannot be sure regarding the material condition of believers as intermediate selves, so we cannot be certain about that of unbelievers. We do know, however, from the words of Jesus, that the spiritual state of the lost after death is one of conscious agony, with no hope of release.

This is horrifying indeed. I struggle even to write this. These thoughts should motivate all believers in Christ to engage regularly, compassionately, prayerfully, and biblically about these matters with nonbelievers, especially those we know best, as instructed by the brother of Jesus in Jude 17–23. And these thoughts should stir the hearts and minds of all nonbelievers to seek and receive the saving grace of our Lord Jesus Christ while there is still time.

4

The Resurrected Self

As noted thus far, we started life as the Initial Self, begun at the moment when the sperm and egg from our parents united. Approximately nine months later, at our birth, we began to be the Independent Self. At that time we became detached from our mother's body, and have lived as independent selves to this day.

Some in this independent condition have also entered the life of the In-Christ Self, begun at the time of our new birth, when (and if) we received Jesus Christ as our Savior and Guide forever. After our earthly existence each of us—believer and nonbeliever alike—will become an Intermediate Self, beginning the moment we die. In this condition we will await the next phase of selfhood: the Resurrected Self.

While there is some lack of clarity about our mode and manner of existence in the intermediate state (for example, what kind of body, if any, we will have), there is much less uncertainty about how we will exist as resurrected selves throughout eternity. Following are some very important scriptures about the bodily resurrection, inspired by God and written by his servants specifically for our instruction and encouragement. (Some of these passages are abbreviated due to space considerations, but are most helpful when read in their entirety.)

> But your dead will live, LORD; their bodies will rise—let those who dwell in the dust wake up and shout for joy—your dew is like the dew of the morning; the earth will give birth to her dead. (Isa 26:19)

> Multitudes who sleep in the dust of the earth will awake: some to everlasting life, others to shame and everlasting contempt. Those who are wise will shine like the brightness of the heavens, and those who lead many to righteousness, like the stars for ever and ever. (Dan 12:2–3)

> The people of this age marry and are given in marriage. But those who are considered worthy of taking part in the age to come and in the resurrection from the dead will neither marry nor be given in marriage, and they can no longer die; for they are like the angels. They are God's children, since they are children of the resurrection. (Luke 20:34–36)

> For just as the Father raises the dead and gives them life, even so the Son gives life to whom he is pleased to give it. . . . Very truly I tell you, a time is coming and now has come when the dead will hear the voice of the Son of God and those who hear will live. . . . Do not be amazed at this, for a time is coming when all who are in their graves will hear his voice and come out—those who have done what is good will rise to live, and those who have done what is evil will rise to be condemned. (John 5:21–29)

> When you sow, you do not plant the body that will be, but just a seed, perhaps of wheat or of something else. But God gives it a body as he has determined, and to each kind of seed he gives its own body. . . . So will it be with the resurrection of the dead. The body that is sown is perishable, it is raised imperishable; it is sown in dishonor, it is raised in glory; it is sown in weakness, it is raised in power; it is sown a natural body, it is raised a spiritual body. . . . And just as we have borne the image of the earthly man, so shall we bear the image of the

The Resurrected Self

> heavenly man. . . . Listen, I tell you a mystery: We shall not all sleep, but we will all be changed—in a flash, in the twinkling of an eye, at the last trumpet. For the trumpet will sound, the dead will be raised imperishable, and we will be changed. (1 Cor 15:37–52)

> After this I looked, and there before me was a great multitude that no one could count, from every nation, tribe, people and language, standing before the throne and before the Lamb. They were wearing white robes and were holding palm branches in their hands. . . . "These are they who have come out of the great tribulation; they have washed their robes and made them white in the blood of the Lamb. Therefore they are before the throne of God and serve him day and night in his temple; and he who sits on the throne will shelter them with his presence. Never again will they hunger; never again will they thirst. The sun will not beat down on them, nor any scorching heat. For the Lamb at the center of the throne will be their shepherd; he will lead them to springs of living water. And God will wipe away every tear from their eyes." (Rev 7:9–17)

After reading these extraordinary words concerning our resurrected selves, we who know Christ are left with adoration, wonder, and praise toward God and anticipation for the life to come in our glorified, resurrected bodies. The above scriptures do not tell us all we would like to know, but they reveal all that God wants us to know.

I have been especially blessed over the years to dwell as much about what will *not* be true of our resurrected selves as what *will* be true. I don't care to know if I will be able to fly or be transported in Star Trek fashion from point A to point B. But I care and delight greatly to know that I, and all in God's kingdom, will no longer experience sickness, sadness, or sin in the new heaven and new earth. Of course, the actual, positive presence of God will be the reason why these negatives will never be found in the heavenly glory. They must flee forever from the presence of the One who is perfect in strength, gladness, and holiness.

We will be embodied and perfected even more wonderfully than Adam and Eve in the garden, because we will be united with God, in Christ, in a way that our first parents were not. Even now we "may participate in the divine nature" (2 Pet 1:4). How much more will this be true throughout eternity.

Some Will Be Translated

In connection with the Resurrected Self, we should mention the translation (sometimes called the rapture) of all persons living on earth at the time of Christ's return, mentioned in 1 Thess 4:13–18. Here we read that when Jesus returns, "God will bring with Jesus those who have fallen asleep in him. . . . For the Lord himself will come down from heaven . . . and the dead in Christ will rise first. After that, we who are still alive and are left will be caught up [Latin *rapiemur*] together with them in the clouds to meet the Lord in the air. And so we will be with the Lord forever."

Does this Bible passage compel us to denote another distinct self—the translated self? For multitudes of people—all Christ-followers alive when Jesus returns—this will surely bring about a new way of being. In reply, I see no need to list a distinctly new self, because this study of our different selves is covering only believers as a whole and unbelievers as a whole. It seems best, therefore, to consider these translated saints as a sub-set of the resurrected—that is, fully glorified—selves.

Strictly speaking, because these believers will not have died, they will not be resurrected, but will be transformed and glorified, receiving their eternal bodies at the time Jesus returns, along with the resurrected believers. The raptured believers will not experience the Intermediate Self; they will be changed from their earthly selves directly to their glorified selves.

While there is *much* debate about the timing of this translation or resurrection event, there is no debate among Bible believers about the certainty of it. Our theories and arguments about when the translation will occur, especially whether it will take place before or after a time of terrible distress and tribulation, will

The Resurrected Self

not influence God's decision on the matter. Our fervent hopes and desires, however, should be ever in tune with the longings of the first-century believers: "Come, Lord Jesus" (Rev 22:20); "Come, Lord!" (1 Cor 16:22).

Will Our Resurrected Body Be Physically Linked to Our Earthly Body?

Before moving to a consideration of our final two selves, we raise one more issue pertaining to the Resurrected Self: Will there be a physical, material link of some kind between a person's resurrected body and the body they had while on earth, and if so, what is the nature of that connection?

What does it mean to say that the dead—those alive in the afterworld right now—will rise someday? Why does God need to do this work of raising them? Can't God just create a totally new body for them when he chooses at some later time, perhaps from a blueprint or DNA pattern stored in his omniscient mind? Why does it have to be a resurrected body? What does that even mean, especially for those who have been dead for hundreds or thousands of years? Is there a physical "germ" or molecule that God will take from the earthly body and grow it into a resurrected body?

I once heard of an exhumation after the deceased had been dead for a very long time. When the workers opened the burial vault they found nothing but very fine dust. "Ashes to ashes, dust to dust." At the resurrection, will God take a bit of that dust and form a new body?

What about those whose ashes were scattered over a mountainside, as my father's ashes were, or those who were buried at sea and consumed by sea creatures, or the very poor who were buried without a casket, whose bodies were totally absorbed by dozens of plants and organisms? How important is the continuity—the material connection—between the earthly body and the heavenly body?

In our thinking on these matters, might it help to compare the resurrection of the body (at least in some sense) to the creative activity of God in Eden when he took the dust of the ground, shaped it, and breathed into it the breath of life, thus bringing Adam into existence? God does not have a physical body with hands and lungs, and, as pure spirit, does not actually touch and mold soil physically, or breathe. Is the Genesis account therefore simply using figurative, pictorial language to emphasize that God is our Creator, the one who chose at a certain time, by an act of his will, to bring human beings into existence? Similarly, is the resurrection of the dead God's way of referring to his new creative physical activity in the end times?

Not a lot of theologians and Bible commentators look closely at these questions, if they raise them at all. This is perhaps because this knotty set of issues involves too much speculation, and is best left alone. Some might even consider such questions beneath their dignity to discuss. I was pleased to find some writers, however, who do address the concerns raised here, and I will summarize the views of four (the first two briefly): Augustus Strong, Millard Erickson, Wayne Grudem, and Randy Alcorn.[1] While I will not present the views of others, I should mention that some very worthwhile discussions of certain aspects of our topic are found in the works of Peter Toon, Jerry Walls, and N. T. Wright.[2]

Each of the writers I will summarize here, as would be expected, works with the pertinent words of the Apostle Paul in 1 Cor 15, quoted above, likening the earthly body to seed that is planted in the ground, which is then grown into a new form of life.

Both Strong and Erickson say there is some connection and continuity between the old and new bodies, but we are not able to comprehend the nature of that link. These do not insist on the very same material substance being used, although Strong says there will be "some sort of physical connection between the body that now is and the body that shall be." He continues: "What that physical connection is, it is vain to speculate. We only teach that, though there may not be a single material particle in the new that was

---

1. See Strong, *Systematic Theology*; Erickson, *Christian Theology*; Grudem, *Systematic Theology*; Alcorn, *Heaven*.

2. Toon, *Heaven and Hell*; Walls, *Heaven, Hell, and Purgatory*; and Wright, *Surprised by Hope*.

The Resurrected Self

present in the old, yet there will be such a physical connection that it can be said: 'the new has grown out of the old'... 'this mortal has put on immortality.'"[3]

Grudem goes much further than Strong. Working from Paul's analogy of the seed sown in the ground, he insists:

> W*hatever remains in the grave from our own physical bodies* will be taken by God and transformed and used to make a new resurrection body. But the details of how that will happen remain unclear to us, since Scripture does not specify them—we are to affirm this because Scripture teaches it, even if we cannot fully explain how it can happen....
>
> Someone may object that some bodies completely decay, are absorbed into plants, and then eventually into other bodies, so that nothing of the first body can be found. But in response we must simply say that God can keep track of enough of the elements from each body to form a seed from which to form a new body.... The God who created the universe and created each one of us... can certainly keep track of the parts of our physical bodies that he wishes to preserve and use as the "seed" from which a new body will be made.[4]

Grudem also argues for his conclusion, while admitting that this evidence is suggestive rather than conclusive. He points to the account in Matthew's Gospel that when Jesus died, the tombs also were opened and many *bodies* of the saints who had fallen asleep were raised, and coming out of the tombs after his resurrection they went into the holy city and appeared to many (Matt 27:50–53). Since these came out of their graves after the resurrection of Jesus, Grudem (building on the work of D. A. Carson[5]), concludes: "We may assume that these also were saints who had

---

3. Strong, *Systematic Theology*, 1020. Erickson, *Christian Theology*, 1204–6.

4. Grudem, *Systematic Theology*, 834–35.

5. Carson, *Matthew*, 581–82.

received resurrection bodies as a kind of foretaste of the final day of glorification when Christ returns."[6]

Alcorn, in his longer discussion of these matters, expounds the same ideas as Grudem, and even though he does not directly answer the question whether there will be a material link between the bodies, he clearly believes that there will be. He writes, "We will never be all that God intended for us to be until body and spirit are again joined in resurrection," and then quotes from the Westminster Confession: "All the dead shall be raised up, with the self-same bodies and none other."

Alcorn notes that one Bible teacher, after reading the first printing of his (Alcorn's) book, *Heaven*, expressed his disagreement with Alcorn's belief that there will be a fundamental continuity between our present bodies and our resurrection bodies. "His understanding is that our resurrection bodies will not be earthly, as our present bodies are. He believes they will not contain DNA or any genetic or physical ties to our current bodies."

In reply, Alcorn considers Paul's comparison between Adam's human body and Christ's human body. Adam's body was from the dust of the earth, and Christ's body was from the lineage of Adam. Even today, after his resurrection, Christ *is*—not merely was—a descendant of Adam. He is the last Adam. He is also a descendant of Abraham and David. "Christ's resurrection and glorification did not negate his genetic tie to his ancestors. They do not mean he is no longer a Jew, no longer of Abraham's seed, or no longer fully human. He who is tied to the earth in terms of his humanity will rule the earth for eternity." Alcorn continues:

> One Bible student told me that he couldn't believe that the risen Christ might have DNA. But why not? Who created DNA in the first place? Christ explicitly said that his [resurrection] body was of flesh and bones. Flesh and bones have DNA. . . . [Christ] remains, and will always remain, an actual physical descendant of Abraham and David.[7]

---

6. Grudem, *Systematic Theology*, 833–35.
7. Alcorn, *Heaven*, 116–23.

The Resurrected Self

The implication from Alcorn's statements—even though he does not say this directly—is that, since our bodily resurrection will be like that of Jesus, everyone after their resurrection will continue to have the DNA they had while on earth. If that is so, Thai people will live on as Thais, Nigerians as Nigerians, and Scottish folks as Scots.

It is understandable that some may think that Alcorn is pushing matters too far, especially after we engage in a close reading of 1 Cor 15 with its emphasis on the *spiritual* nature of the resurrection body, but at least Alcorn is willing to consider the topic seriously and reverently. He *does* emphasize the *spiritual* character of our risen bodies, but (rightly, I believe) sees no reason why our spiritual, incorruptible bodies cannot be one with our glorified *human* bodies, just as Christ lives in glory even now. With these thoughts in mind, we will close this fascinating discussion of our resurrected selves with the following encouraging words from Randy Alcorn.

> Scripture portrays resurrection as involving both fundamental continuity and significant dissimilarity. We dare not minimize the dissimilarities—for our glorification will certainly involve a dramatic and marvelous transformation. But, in my experience, the great majority of Christians have underemphasized continuity. They end up thinking of our transformed selves as no longer being ourselves, and the transformed Earth as no longer being the earth. In some cases they view the glorified Christ as no longer being the same Jesus who walked the earth—a belief that early Christians recognized as heresy. . . .
>
> Many of us look forward to Heaven more now than we did when our bodies functioned well. Joni Eareckson Tada says it well: "Somewhere in my broken, paralyzed body is the seed of what I shall become. The paralysis makes what I am to become all the more grand when you contrast atrophied, useless legs against splendorous resurrected legs. I'm convinced that if there are mirrors in heaven (and why not?), the image I'll see will be unmistakably 'Joni,' although a much better, brighter Joni."

Ever Moving On

Inside your body, even if it is failing, is the blueprint for your resurrection body. You may not be satisfied with your current body or mind—but you'll be thrilled with your resurrection upgrades. With them you'll be better able to serve and glorify God and enjoy an eternity of wonders he has prepared for you.[8]

---

8. Alcorn, *Heaven*, 124.

5

The Judged Self and the Eternal Self
Unbelievers

THERE ARE TWO MORE selves that we must (sadly) consider to conclude our remarks concerning the self who dies apart from God: the Judged Self and the Eternal Self of the unbeliever. These two selves come so closely together that it is possible to think of them as practically one, but we will consider them separately, since the judgment is the gateway event into eternity, just as the judgment of believers will lead into their everlasting state. The Judged Self is likely a brief phase of existence, whereas the Eternal Self is everlasting.

I take no pleasure in writing about the future of the lost. Rather, I sorrow greatly, as many readers will do in reading these words. But this is part of the whole will of God (Acts 20:27) that must be proclaimed if we wish to be faithful to our Lord. It has been said often, rightly so, that Jesus—the most loving and kind human being who ever lived—spoke more about hell than any other biblical character.

Those who did not respond affirmatively to God's gracious tug on their hearts during their lifetimes—at whatever level(s) of revelation God was working to enlighten and draw them (John 1:9; 3:17; 12:32–36; Rom 1:18–20; 2:4; Titus 2:11; 2 Pet 3:9)—will be judged at the Great White Throne Judgment described in the last book of the Bible:

> Then I saw a great white throne and him who was seated on it. . . . And I saw the dead, great and small, standing before the throne, and books were opened. Another book was opened, which is the book of life. The dead were judged according to what they had done as recorded in the books. The sea gave up the dead that were in it, and death and Hades gave up the dead that were in them, and each person was judged according to what they had done. Then death and Hades were thrown into the lake of fire. The lake of fire is the second death. Anyone whose name was not found written in the book of life was thrown into the lake of fire. (Rev 20:11–15)

The lost are those who in life ignored, suppressed, or rejected God's voice, whether that voice came through nature, conscience, Scripture, experience, relationships, or other means. These are much like the ones Jesus referred to while lamenting over the city of Jerusalem:

> Jerusalem, Jerusalem, you who kill the prophets and stone those sent to you, how often I have longed to gather your children together as a hen gathers her chicks under her wings, and you were not willing. (Luke 13:34; see also vss 23–30)

> As he approached Jerusalem and saw the city, he wept over it and said, "If you, even you, had only known on this day what would bring you peace—but now it is hidden from your eyes. . . . They [your enemies] will not leave one stone on another, because you did not recognize the time of God's coming to you." (Luke 19:41–44)

There will be degrees of punishment for the lost (as well as degrees of reward for the saved), and the Lord will be completely just and detailed in this aspect of his judgment. Those who on earth directed human trafficking operations, or led human beheading campaigns, or cheated the poor out of their life savings,

The Judged Self and the Eternal Self: Unbelievers

for example, will be judged more severely than those who refrained from such extreme forms of evil.

Twice in the above text from Rev 20 we read that the dead were judged according to what they had done. Other key scriptures reveal this crucial, often overlooked, truth (Eccl 12:14; Matt 11:20–24; 12:36–37; Luke 12:2–3, 47–48; 20:47). There is no one-size-fits-all experience for unbelievers (or believers) in eternity. Each one will be considered personally, fairly, and righteously.

After the judgment the lost will be sent away from God's presence forever. This last phase of life for the unbeliever is The Eternal Self. The most graphic description of the unbeliever in eternity is found in the account, referred to earlier, concerning a rich man and a beggar in the afterlife (Luke 16:19–31). Jesus himself spoke these words, and they are truly heartbreaking.

This biblical text is not, however, the only scripture presenting the awful reality to come for the unsaved. Also from the lips of Jesus we read these statements in his account of the sheep and the goats—those on his right and his left. "Then he will say to those on his left, 'Depart from me, you who are cursed, into the eternal fire prepared for the devil and his angels. . . . Then they will go away to eternal punishment, but the righteous to life eternal'" (Matt 25:41, 46; see also Matt 23:33; Luke 12:4–5, 8–9; 13:23–30; John 8:21–24; 2 Thess 1:7–10; Rev 20:14–15).[1]

∼

In light of these solemn teachings, what should we think of deathbed conversions? By this term we refer to those events when persons who know they are to die very soon appear to turn to Christ, especially after being urged to do so by a friend or relative. I find the following words of Charles Spurgeon to be insightful concerning such experiences:

> Deathbed repentances are hard to estimate; we must leave them with God. But it is a sorrowful fact that those

---

1. Crockett, *Four Views on Hell*, presents literal, metaphorical, purgatorial, and conditional perspectives. In Edwards and Stott, *Evangelical Essentials*, 312–20, John Stott also argues for the conditional (annihilationist) view.

which seemed to be deathbed repentances have seldom turned out to be worth anything when the men have recovered. In fact, I do not remember a case in which the person who recovered has been at all what he said he would be when he thought that he was on the borders of the grave. So you see, suffering is no help to repentance, and it may be a hindrance.

My own conviction is that [deathbed repentances] have been very, very, very, very, very few. We read in Scripture of only one who was saved at the last—the dying thief on the cross. And it has been well said that there was one that none might despair, but only one that none might presume.[2]

The lost person will have experienced six major crisis points before moving into the loneliness of eternity: conception, birth, death, resurrection, judgment, and dismissal. "I never knew you. Away from me, you evildoers" (Matt 7:23). We may be very, very thankful for the words of Abraham some four thousand years ago: "Will not the Judge of all the earth do right" (Gen 18:25)? God will always judge rightly and truthfully, because he alone can see the deepest thoughts and intentions of every person's heart (Deut 32:4; Jer 17:9–10; Luke 16:31; Heb 4:12–13). As George MacDonald said, and is often quoted, "There are only two kinds of people in the end: Those who say to God, 'Thy will be done,' and those to whom God says, in the end, 'Thy will be done.'"

God will never send anyone away who comes to him, at whatever age, as a little child, in humility and trust. As Jesus said so beautifully, "Let the little children come to me, and do not hinder them, for the kingdom of God belongs to such as these" (Mark 10:4; see also Matt 11:25–30).

---

2. Carter, *2200 Quotations*, 175.

6

The Judged Self

Believers

WE ARE MOVING ON in our consideration of "the self"—who and what a person is at their core. You and I are unique selves, as are all who live, and have lived, on the earth. We exist individually, even though we are part of a certain cultural milieu that shapes our thinking and behaviors hugely, whether or not we realize the ways or degrees to which we are influenced. Within this cultural conditioning, each of us moves through life as a unique person—a unique Self who experiences a number of overlapping, subsidiary "selves" through time and into eternity.

This chapter and the two following concern genuine believers—the redeemed of all ages. These are now either (1) living in heavenly glory as intermediate selves, or (2) living on earth, awaiting either their entrance into the intermediate state through death, or their translation (rapture) if they are alive when Jesus returns. In either case, our final two selves will be the Judged Self and the Eternal Self (using the same category names as for unbelievers).

With regard to the judgment of believers, theologians have different opinions as to when the saved will be judged and whether different groups of believers will be judged at different times, and on what specific bases. These are interesting questions to think about, but for our purposes here it seems best (and simplest) to consider all believers—past, present, future—under the broad category of the Judgment Seat of Christ, which may be thought of as one aspect of the Great White Throne Judgment (Rev 20:11–15). (We will say more about this below.) The two chief Bible texts on the Judgment Seat of Christ are from the Apostle Paul:

> By the grace God has given me, I laid a foundation as a wise builder, and someone else is building on it. But each one should build with care. For no one can lay any foundation other than the one already laid, which is Jesus Christ. If anyone builds on this foundation using gold, silver, costly stones, wood, hay or straw, their work will be shown for what it is, because the Day will bring it to light. It will be revealed with fire, and the fire will test the quality of each person's work. If what has been built survives, the builder will receive a reward. If it is burned up, the builder will suffer loss but yet will be saved—even though only as one escaping through the flames. (1 Cor 3:10–15)

> Therefore we are always confident and know that as long as we are at home in the body we are away from the Lord. For we live by faith, not by sight. We are confident, I say, and would prefer to be away from the body and at home with the Lord. So we make it our goal to please him, whether we are at home in the body or away from it. For we must all appear before the judgment seat of Christ, so that each of us may receive what is due us for the things done while in the body, whether good or bad. (2 Cor 5:6–11)

Two Major Judgment Events?

Some writers and preachers distinguish between the Judgment Seat of Christ and the Great White Throne Judgment. Those who make this distinction emphasize that the former is for believers only, and is not a judgment to determine who will be saved, since those being judged here have all been redeemed and forgiven through the

The Judged Self: Believers

atoning sacrifice of Jesus Christ, even if many of these lived before Christ's crucifixion. They are being judged to determine rewards or loss of rewards based on how they lived and served the Lord since they came to know him.

Those judged at the Great White Throne Judgment, it is said, are unbelievers, and are judged ultimately on the basis of their response to God's revelation and grace shown to them while on earth, and how they lived in light of their overall attitude toward God, themselves, and others.

While these two groups and two kinds of judgment activity are clearly taught in the Bible, the names for these two judgments do not necessarily indicate two separate occasions. It may be, of course, that these judgments will occur at two different times, with the focus of each as just indicated, but it is also possible, as mentioned previously, that they may occur in one comprehensive last judgment (the Great White Throne Judgment) with the Judgment Seat of Christ as part of this mighty event. At this immense occasion, the judgment of unbelievers and believers, as well as the judgment of nations (sheep and goats) (Matt 25:31–46) and of fallen angels (2 Pet 2:4; Jude 6) would take place.

After studying numerous biblical passages on God's future judgment activity, I have come to believe—but cannot insist—that there will be one final judgment event just before the beginning of the eternal state, with different emphases and particular groups in view.

I have even wondered at times if the Judgment Seat of Christ is not only one big occasion for all believers gathered together after Christ returns, especially to receive rewards, but is also something that takes place sooner, privately, alone with our Lord, just after each child of God dies. Whether or not this will be so, I will surely be in awe if I ever hear—as I long to hear—Jesus say to me, while he looks intently into my eyes, "Well done, good and faithful servant. . . . Enter into the joy of your Lord" (Matt 25:21, NKJV).

Amazingly, on another note, we who trust in the Lord will, in some sense, assist him in the awesome responsibility of judging both humans and angels (1 Cor 6:2–3; also see Rev 20:4). As the people of God, after our individual judgment (whenever that will be), we will personally assist our Lord in his work of judgment. We await the coming great "Day" (culminating activity) when we will be both judged and judges.

On What Basis Will Believers Be Judged?

We need not be concerned about whether we will be qualified to judge (or rule) others rightly. God will see that we are. But we are to be concerned about our day in court, as individual Christians. This is rarely, if ever, preached or mentioned in devotional literature or other Christian writing.

Perhaps this failure is because we (Christian leaders, pastors, laypersons, and writers alike) focus so much on comforting the afflicted (ourselves and others) that we neglect to join with God in his serious work of afflicting the comfortable (ourselves and others), whether we experience God's affliction during this life (Heb 12:4–17) or when we stand before him in judgment, assuming (rightly, I believe) that we may speak of his merciful chastisement at that time, if there will be such, as benevolent but necessary affliction.

We may not understand how God will, in part, judge his redeemed ones negatively, while at the same time (or thereafter) reward us and usher us into everlasting blessedness. However, this does not justify the widespread avoidance of teaching on the relevant scriptures (see the following) and their implications. I am convinced that the loving sternness of God toward his precious children needs to be preached today, and can be preached and taught with the same combination of directness and mercy as Jesus himself would display if he were on earth today.

A close reading of Matt 5–7 and Rev 1–3 will instruct us on how Jesus blends these essential qualities beautifully in his work as the master teacher and pastor. I am convinced, in addition, that God's Holy Spirit will lead us into the truth on this matter, discerning what God wants us to know, not only doctrinally but also personally, concerning our present way of life in view of our

The Judged Self: Believers

coming individual judgment, when we sincerely ask him to do so (Luke 11:13; John 16:12–15).

God's basis for our judgment as individual believers, as best as I can discern, will be our faithfulness to the total pattern of godly living and serving according to the whole of biblical teaching, as we learned progressively of this divine pattern throughout our individual life situations. The more we came to know, the more we became responsible to follow.

This range of living and serving, for which we will be judged, will include such matters as responsible stewardship of our talents and gifts, fervent and consistent love for God, radical love and justice for our neighbors as ourselves, serious involvement in fulfilling the great commission, genuine forgiveness of those who have harmed us, and robust holiness of life: thoughts, words, and actions.

It is frequently said that true Christians will not be judged for their sins, since these were paid for at Calvary, but we will be judged regarding our works as believers. While this teaching has grounding in important biblical revelation (John 5:24; 1 John 2:1–2), we cannot and should not try to isolate our sins as believers from our works as believers.

You may, for example, spend valuable hours each month volunteering at the local food pantry and used clothing store. This is surely good work because it helps many needy people. But if you do this primarily or even partially to avoid more difficult responsibilities at home, such as intentionally training your children in matters of Christian truth and Christian living, your sin of avoidance (omission) tarnishes your good work of helping the poor. Many such examples could be given.

The sins of believers are of major concern to God. They not only mar our good works, but they grieve God, and will be taken into account when we stand before him at the end of our earthly lives. Both our righteous actions, words, thoughts, and motives, as well as our unrighteous ones, will be brought out into the full light of God's courtroom when he judges his redeemed. The same will be true of both our surrender or stubbornness toward God's will in both the little and big issues of life.

Sometimes God does not wait for the ultimate judgment event of believers, but (in great sadness, for sure) takes action—even ending our lives—when we continue to live in disobedience to him. (On this crucial point, please read, seriously, alone, 1 Cor 11:27–32, one of the most shocking texts in the Bible regarding God's hatred of sin in the lives of his people.)

Furthermore, one sin that God must hate (and awaits his judgment) is the choice of preachers and others who know the contents of the Bible to deliberately avoid referring to such scriptures as the one just mentioned in order to grow their church, or not to offend people, or not to have friends turn away from them. "Not many of you should become teachers, my fellow believers, because you know that we who teach will be judged more strictly" (Jas 3:1). "If anyone is ashamed of me and my words in this adulterous and sinful generation, the Son of Man will be ashamed of them when he comes in his Father's glory with the holy angels" (Mark 8:38).

Urgent Scriptures on God's Judgment

Some highly instructive Bible texts, in addition to those quoted earlier from 1 Cor 3 and 2 Cor 5, will be valuable for each of us to contemplate seriously as we ponder God's judgment of believers, especially ourselves—each of us personally. Some of these passages apply to unbelievers as well as God's children, but they are listed here mainly for their application to the people of God.

> Now all has been heard; here is the conclusion of the matter: Fear God and keep his commandments, for this is the duty of all mankind. For God will bring every deed into judgment, including every hidden thing, whether it is good or evil. (Eccl 12:13–14)

> Then those who feared the LORD talked with each other, and the LORD listened and heard. A scroll of remembrance was written in his presence concerning those who feared the LORD and honored his name. "On the day when I act," says the Lord Almighty, "they will be my treasured possession." (Mal 3:16–17)

The Judged Self: Believers

For the mouth speaks what the heart is full of. A good man brings good things out of the good stored up in him, and an evil man brings evil things out of the evil stored up in him. But I tell you that everyone will have to give account on the day of judgment for every empty word they have spoken. For by your words you will be acquitted, and by your words you will be condemned. (Matt 12:34–37)

For the Son of Man is going to come in his Father's glory with his angels, and then he will reward each person according to what they have done. (Matt 16:27)

Blessed are you when people hate you, when they exclude you and insult you and reject your name as evil, because of the Son of Man. Rejoice in that day and leap for joy, because great is your reward in heaven. For that is how their ancestors treated the prophets. (Luke 6:22–23)

From everyone who has been given much, much will be demanded; and from the one who has been entrusted with much, much more will be asked. (Luke 12:48)

Moreover, the Father judges no one, but has entrusted all judgment to the Son . . . (John 5:22)

For none of us lives for ourselves alone, and none of us dies for ourselves alone. . . . You, then, why do you judge your brother or sister? Or why do you treat them with contempt? For we will all stand before God's judgment seat. It is written: "As surely as I live," says the Lord, "every knee will bow before me; every tongue will acknowledge God." So then, each of us will give an account of ourselves to God. (Rom 14:7, 10–12)

The one who plants and the one who waters have one purpose, and they will each be rewarded according to their own labor. (1 Cor 3:8)

I care very little if I am judged by you or by any human court; indeed, I do not even judge myself. My conscience is clear, but that does not make me innocent. It is the Lord who judges me. Therefore judge nothing before the appointed time; wait until the Lord comes. He will bring to light what is hidden in darkness and will expose the motives of the heart. At that time each will receive their praise from God. (1 Cor 4:3-5)

Whatever you do, work at it with all your heart, as working for the Lord, not for human masters, since you know that you will receive an inheritance from the Lord as a reward. It is the Lord Christ you are serving. (Col 3:23-24)

[The] time for my departure is near. I have fought the good fight, I have finished the race, I have kept the faith. Now there is in store for me the crown of righteousness, which the Lord, the righteous Judge, will award to me on that day—and not only to me, but also to all who have longed for his appearing. (2 Tim 4:6-8)

God is not unjust; he will not forget your work and the love you have shown him as you have helped his people and continue to help them. (Heb 6:10)

Just as people are destined to die once, and after that to face judgment, so Christ was sacrificed once to take away the sins of many; and he will appear a second time, not to bear sin, but to bring salvation to those who are waiting for him. (Heb 9:27-28)

And now, dear children, continue in him, so that when he appears we may be confident and unashamed before him at his coming. (1 John 2:28)

God is love. Whoever lives in love lives in God, and God in them. This is how love is made complete among us so that we will have confidence on the day of judgment: In this world we are like Jesus. There is no fear in love. But perfect love drives out fear, because fear has to do with punishment. The one who fears is not made perfect in love. (1 John 4:16-18)

Watch out that you do not lose what we have worked for, but that you may be rewarded fully. (2 John 8)

And I heard a voice speaking from heaven. It said, "Write as follows: 'Blessed are the dead who die in the Lord from this time onward. Yes, says the Spirit, let them rest from

The Judged Self: Believers

their labors; for what they have done goes with them.'"
(Rev 14:13, Weymouth)

Look, I am coming soon! My reward is with me, and I will give to each person according to what they have done. (Rev 22:12)

These are remarkable scriptures indeed. How much there is to ponder deeply, and to apply. Those who know and walk closely with Jesus Christ as their Savior and Lord are the most blessed of all inhabitants of the earth. We have nothing to fear, either in this life or in the life to come. The above text from 1 John 4 states, "There is no fear in love." If we live in the God who is love, "we will have confidence on the day of judgment."

This confidence will not be based on our having lived sinless lives. Far from it. But it will be ours because we have, regularly and increasingly over the years, received God's gracious paternal forgiveness (in contrast to his judicial forgiveness at the time of our justification) whenever he convicted us of wrongdoing and we confessed our sin to him (1 John 1:5—2:2). It has been well-said that "the most important minutes in the life of a Christian are the five minutes after we sin." Unconfessed sin, over time, will devastate a believer: body, soul, and spirit.

So much more could be said here about the judgment of God's people—those who have been redeemed by the blood of the Lamb for all eternity. What are the rewards we will receive, for example, and how should this major New Testament theme affect our daily lives? This is an important though little-emphasized consideration that, I believe, should be on our minds regularly. For this reason we now move to investigate the issue of rewards for believers after this earthly life.

7

The Judged Self

Rewards for Believers

As a long-time student of the Bible—along with millions of such ones over the centuries—I noticed frequently the large number of scripture references presenting the truth that faithful children of God will be rewarded when they stand before God after they complete their service on earth.

Who would not be aware of this prominent biblical teaching? R. C. Sproul has noted that "there are at least twenty-five occasions where the New Testament clearly teaches that we will be granted rewards according to our works."[1]

However, even with this awareness in the back of my mind, I seldom brought the theme of rewards into my active consciousness, as something to think much about. I was thankful for the biblical teaching on this aspect of the afterlife, but I was not motivated by God's promises of rewards and crowns to live well and do good, except that I greatly longed to hear Jesus say, "Well done, good and faithful servant, enter into the joy of your Lord." To me, this was all I needed to keep going. Just to hear these words and see Jesus smile at me was all I ever longed for and hoped for.

---

1. Quoted by Wilkinson, *Life God Rewards*, 122.

The Judged Self: Rewards for Believers

A very big part of my thinking on the grace of God toward me—whether in my initial salvation, Christian life and service, or eternal blessedness—has been that I am and have always been, in myself, a very unworthy person, deserving not a single one of God's kindnesses or gifts. I deserve, rather, condemnation and punishment for my sins in all dimensions: thoughts, words, actions, sins of omission, commission, and disposition, sins of self-preoccupation, harm, and neglect toward others, and disregard of biblical teachings that make me uncomfortable.

The idea of *deserving* rewards for anything good that I have done or said or thought, or not done or said or thought, has always been foreign to my way of thinking, even repugnant.

From the early years of my Christian life I have had a very strong and very biblical sense of sin and sins—especially mine—as the most heinous of all human and angelic activities. Such an estimation of human nature and wrongdoing is, I fully realize, repugnant to many people. They believe, or make themselves believe, that people are naturally good. The root of this belief, I am convinced, is that they do not want to believe that they personally are flawed or bad in any serious sense.

They may point to instances such as neighbors (or themselves) coming to the aid of a local family in great need after a tornado or fire destroyed their home, or when the main breadwinner of the family was tragically killed. While such acts of kindness are genuinely praiseworthy, they do not establish a doctrine of universal human goodness. Heroes often say when they are being interviewed, "I just did what anyone would have done."

Even though not everyone would have offered the needed assistance, many would, and we are all grateful for such kind souls. But the truth about human nature, which many—even nonreligious folks—know to be true is that human beings, especially (but not only) when raised with little or no proper direction, are essentially selfish, prideful, and seeking their own benefit and pleasure above all else, even if this means violating whatever inner restraint they may have.

Ever Moving On

I include myself in this grand indictment of the human species. The sin of our first parents presented in the third chapter of the Bible changed human nature drastically. What God said was "very good" (using a very strong Hebrew term in Gen 1:31)—namely, all of his creation—was horribly altered by human disobedience (and, before that, by angelic disobedience). We have all been affected adversely by sin, even as biblically informed theologians rightly speak of original sin and actual sin.

My understanding of human sinfulness, however, is not based primarily on the ideas of theologians or church tradition, but on three lines of thought. First, the divinely inspired scriptures speak of our pervasive human corruption frequently and forcefully (Gen 6:5; 8:21; Pss 4:1–3; 143:2; Prov 20:9; Eccl 7:20; Rom 3:10–12, 23; 5:12; Gal 3:22; Eph 2:1–3; 1 John 5:19). A quiet and thoughtful reading of these texts will grip a person (for the first time or during subsequent readings) with the solemn truth of human depravity.

I will quote only one text as typical of many, found in the book of the prophet Jeremiah: "The heart is deceitful above all things and beyond cure. Who can understand it?" (17:9). Along with the major themes of God's extensive and intensive goodness and mercy, the Bible presents the major themes of humanity's extensive and intensive selfishness and abusiveness toward others, and defiance of God.

A second line of thought—my study of human history and activities, past and present—reveals the horrendous evils of dictators and multitudes of powerful people (as well as ordinary people) with regard to violence, greed, slavery, economic injustice, sexual abuse and trafficking, stigmatization and coercion of all kinds, selfishness, and arrogance toward God. Such study not only confirms the biblical teachings but leaves me with no lasting hope for this sinful world apart from the grace and mercy of God when people respond to him in humility, repentance, and childlike faith.

The third factor leading to my firm conclusion about human sinfulness, and anyone's deservedness of rewards and crowns, is a very personal one: my memory of who I am and have been

The Judged Self: Rewards for Believers

throughout my life keeps me mindful of how and how often I have grieved the God of all righteousness, holiness, mercy, and love.

Such memory and awareness, I am grateful to say, does not burden me with guilt, shame, or grief, because I am assured that my sins have been forgiven and covered through the cross of Christ. However, when I add this personal knowledge of myself to the factors of biblical teaching and human conduct throughout human history to the present day, I adhere strongly to the truth of human corruption—both innate and actual. How can a person think of God's grace and mercy being deserved in any sense, not to mention God's *rewarding* of people—even redeemed ones—after they die?

Thinking Seriously of Rewards

During the 1990s, while I was serving on the theology faculty of Bethel Seminary in Minnesota, I attended a very stimulating and somewhat provocative seminary chapel service. The speaker was Dr. Earl Radmacher, then president of Western Seminary in Oregon. He gave a solid, biblically based presentation on the topic of rewards after we die—a subject I had never heard anyone expound on before—and then invited attenders to respond.

I left chapel that day challenged but unsure of his proposal. He argued that God's people need to see the Bible's bold teaching on this issue in a new light. The scriptural teaching that we will be rewarded is intended to motivate us to serve God and others faithfully and diligently.

We must realize that notwithstanding whatever good we may do we will remain only "unprofitable servants." Yet we also know that it is the Lord himself who encourages us and exhorts us to work, specifically in order to receive rewards in the next life. Of course, our highest motivation is to honor and glorify God in all that we do. But it is also important to labor for rewards, because they will carry over into eternity, for all eternity.

As the years passed, I probably thought about that chapel service as much or more than any other during my years of teaching at the seminary. But, I was still reluctant to accept Radmacher's proposal as a motivating factor in my life and service. I was still hesitant because of my unworthiness, even though I knew I was justified and already glorified in his sight, as are all genuine Christians (Rom 8:30). The idea of earning or deserving rewards, as I saw it, had no place in my theology. Yet the biblical passages, such as those listed earlier in this chapter, continued to surface in my personal and vocational reading of the scriptures.

In 2016 I purchased a little book, *A Life God Rewards*, by Bruce Wilkinson, author of the best-seller, *The Prayer of Jabez*. I bought it because of the title and the topic, which continued to reappear in my thinking since the chapel service twenty or more years earlier. The words on the cover accurately describe the contents: Why Everything You Do Today Matters Forever.

In this work, Wilkinson acknowledged the influence of Earl Radmacher and a number of other prominent scholars as they interacted with and debated his (Wilkinson's) study materials on rewards. They encouraged him to fine-tune and develop his ideas even further. *A Life God Rewards* is the result of a weeklong graduate course at Western Seminary, taught by Wilkinson at Radmacher's invitation, and during which the invited scholars and many others attended.

Regarding this week, Wilkinson wrote the following:

> One day a church historian from Romania assured us that what we were studying was not new theology; it had been part of Christian beliefs and teaching from the first century on. To make his point he asked us, "What do the greats of church history such as Augustine, Luther, Calvin, Wesley, and Spurgeon all have in common?" When everyone hesitated, he told us his answer: "They all earnestly believed in and hoped for eternal rewards."[2]

Having read Wilkinson's book twice, I understand and believe with my head what he and the luminaries he quotes seem to be saying. First, God will give rewards to his faithful servants

---

2. Wilkinson, *Life God Rewards*, 12–13; cf. Alcorn, *Heaven*, 68, 215–35, 470.

The Judged Self: Rewards for Believers

in proportion to the quantity and quality of their good works on earth. Second, the biblical teachings on rewards are meant to motivate us to serve our Lord obediently, for rewards, throughout our lives, no matter how great the opposition, persecution, and difficulties we may face. The second point is not as explicit in the book as the former, but it is clearly implied.

As just noted, I have come to believe with my intellect these two aspects of the scriptural view of rewards. It has always been vitally important to me to believe *all* that the written word of God teaches. When I am sure that a doctrinal position is grounded in a balanced, serious study of the whole of biblical revelation, I am compelled (gladly) to accept it as true.

Having said this, however, on the subject of rewards I have yet to experience profoundly in my heart and life—my emotions, thoughts, and will—the full realization of that which I believe in my head. I know of no way to compel myself to be affected more than I am in my heart and soul—so that I actually do this or that in the hope of some eternal reward.

I will admit that as I move through these later years of life (and, yes, through the subtle yet persistent influence of Radmacher, Wilkinson and—above all—the biblical teachings), I am *extremely* grateful for the knowledge that I am, as far as I can know, pleasing God with my life and service for him and others. I am not laboring for rewards, but I am very encouraged by the knowledge that I am bringing joy to the heart of my Best Friend and some elements of help and encouragement to some I know, and (I pray often) to some I don't know.

What, Specifically, Will Be the Rewards?

On a somewhat different yet closely related issue, the most important information I was looking for while reading *A Life God Rewards* had to do with the nature of the rewards we will receive at the judgment, and seemingly retain throughout eternity. I was persuaded that our rewards will involve more than freedom from sin, guilt, pain, and suffering, and more than the broad range of positive blessings that accompanies our full salvation in Christ.

I was also convinced that there are *degrees* of reward for the redeemed just as there are degrees of punishment for the wicked. But I longed to know just what the Bible (and Wilkinson) said our rewards might consist of. It was not enough for me, as a motivating factor to live well and do good, to think of crowns and rewards if I did not have some idea of just what, in particular, I might receive at the judgment.

I was disappointed after reading *A Life God Rewards* that I found nothing specific that appealed to me. This is no fault of the author; I am thankful he did not insist on things that are not in the scriptures. What he did, however, was point out two categories of rewards that *are* found in the Bible, both in the words of Jesus.

The first type is the reward of rulership—more specifically, serving God through rulership. Wilkinson is convinced, from the words and example of Jesus, that "in heaven, we will desperately crave to serve." Because we are servants of God, and will be forever, and because *doing* is a servant's language of devotion, then, "In heaven, more opportunity to do God's will through loving service will be our highest reward." And, "in the upside-down kingdom of heaven, the highest word for serving is *ruling*."

Wilkinson reached this conclusion from the teachings of Jesus. The Lord told his disciples that their reward in heaven for serving him here will be to sit on twelve thrones and judge the tribes of Israel (Matt 19:28). Wilkinson also pointed to the mina parable, in which the highest reward for service was to have authority over ten cities (Luke 19:17). And in the parable of the talents the reward is similar: "I will make you ruler over many things" (Matt 25:21, 23).

Wilkinson emphasizes important qualifications, however, and his words are worth quoting here:

> Ruling in heaven will have *nothing* in common with the corruption and manipulation we're used to seeing in displays of power on earth! When the curse of sin is removed and you and I are restored to our creation purpose [stewardship, Gen 1:28], we will be free to rule for

The Judged Self: Rewards for Believers

God to our fullest powers while bringing only the highest good to ourselves and to others. . . . Serve faithfully here, rule perfectly there.[3]

The second type of reward presented by Wilkinson is treasure—seemingly, some kinds of money and possessions. When the Apostle Peter, after hearing Jesus tell a wealthy young man why he should leave his possessions and follow him ("You will have treasure in heaven," Matt 19:21), Peter asked Jesus, "See, we have left all and followed you. Therefore what shall we have?"

Concerning this account, Wilkinson remarks:

> I love the fact that Jesus didn't scold Peter for his self-interest. Or smile and say, "I wasn't actually *serious* about treasure in heaven." Instead, He gave a most revealing answer. Jesus told Peter that he and the other disciples would rule over the nation of Israel when He set up his kingdom. Then He said that every person who leaves all to follow Him would be repaid a hundredfold (Matt 19:29). A hundredfold is the equivalent of a 10,000 percent return!

When Jesus exhorted his listeners to "lay up for yourselves treasures in heaven" (Matt 6:20), he "was clearly talking about actual treasure and how you can keep it. . . . He didn't reveal what treasure in heaven would look like or how it would be measured, but it *will* be highly valuable." Wilkinson does not believe that the words of Jesus here are meant to teach primarily that *spiritual* rewards in heaven are more important than material ones, as many (probably most) Christians seem to assume they teach.[4]

Some will ask: But why would treasure matter to me in heaven? Wilkinson replies:

> I understand the question. Yet we have to conclude from Jesus' dramatic statements here and elsewhere that our treasure will matter greatly to us in eternity! In God's kingdom, when the sinful pull of greed, envy, and manipulation is absent, we will *enjoy* our treasure, and it

3. Wilkinson, *Life God Rewards*, 62, 73-74.
4. Wilkinson, *Life God Rewards*, 79-81.

will serve a pure and meaningful purpose. . . . [It] will allow us to serve, to give, to accomplish, and to enjoy more for Him.[5]

Furthermore, he notes, in comparison to earthly stewards, "It is not, as you might expect, that you will steward more treasure in heaven, but that you will *own* it" (Luke 16:10–12).[6]

While I struggle with the idea of having some kind of heavenly assets awarded to me for doing well on earth, and having more wealth than some others who didn't serve so faithfully, and less than others who excelled in their labors, I must admit that Wilkinson presents a biblically supported case for there being some kind of material possessions for believers to use in heaven, since our eternal home will be the "new earth"—an actual physical home for all believers from all the years of time.

I'm not sure if I'll be able to buy an autographed, handwritten copy of the book of Exodus from Moses for my library on the new earth, but I am sure that however God plans for us to enjoy him, serve him, and love our neighbors as ourselves will be perfect. Personally, I am not motivated by the rewards of rulership or material possessions. Would I be pleasing God more by my present service if I were so motivated?

Indeed, I suspect that Jesus may have used these two categories of rewards illustratively (as examples of many other categories of rewards) rather than exclusively, in light of the culture of his day, in which ruling and owning treasure would have been phenomenal privileges. I believe, but cannot prove, that even if our rewards will include rulership and actual treasure, there will be other kinds of rewards as well, such as the intensifications of marvelous experiences we enjoy in this life—perhaps music, dining, reading, learning, drama, and skydiving.

However, if God chooses to bless his servants in glory primarily with the rewards of rulership and possessions—these are, after all, the two main categories presented by Jesus—so as to enable us to express our love for him and others in glory, and

---

5. Wilkinson, *Life God Rewards*, 83–88.
6. Wilkinson, *Life God Rewards*, 86.

enjoy life in his heavenly kingdom to the fullest, I will be eternally grateful—literally.

Two choice statements included at the end of Wilkinson's book are worth quoting here:

> *From Charles Stanley.* The kingdom of God will not be the same for all believers. Let me put it another way. Some believers will have rewards for their earthly faithfulness; others will not. Some will reign with Christ; others will not (see 2 Tim 2:12). Some will be rich in the kingdom of God; others will be poor (see Luke 12:21, 33). Some will be given true riches; others will not (see Luke 16:11). Some will be given heavenly treasures of their own; others will not (see Luke 16:12).[7]

> *From C. S. Lewis.* If there lurks in most modern minds the notion that to desire our own good and earnestly to hope for the enjoyment of it is a bad thing, I submit that this notion has crept in from Kant and the Stoics and is no part of the Christian faith. Indeed, if we consider the unblushing promises of reward and the staggering nature of the rewards promised in the Gospels, it would seem that Our Lord finds our desires not too strong, but too weak.[8]

Personal Words on Rewards and Judgment

On a personal note, only recently has the idea of being rewarded affected me more than just cognitively. As indicated, I rarely thought of it throughout most of my Christian life, because I didn't understand why possible rewards, crowns, or some other kinds of honors from God on some future judgment day should additionally motivate me to live and serve rightly. After all, the best of God's servants are only doing what he expects of them and equips them to do. I was very thankful to be able to serve my Savior, and I was very happy doing it.

---

7. Quoted in Wilkinson, *Life God Rewards*, 123–24.
8. Quoted in Wilkinson, *Life God Rewards*, 124.

Ever Moving On

Recently, however, I have struggled with some discouragement about my present service for God and others. I ask myself, does it matter what I am doing? Am I having any real impact on anyone? Why exert myself as I do at this time of difficult health issues? But then I visualize the smile of Jesus—both in the future and in my life now—and sense his present approval of my recent labors, and become aware of his coming rewards and blessings, whatever these will be, and these thoughts propel me beautifully. In my best moments I need no audible words from Jesus or others to be encouraged.

Yet, I regret to say, I have many moments that are not my best. At such times I must remind myself of this new, developing, motivating factor: If I am serving God with diligence, with full reliance on his wisdom and strength, and with purity of heart and motives, then I can be assured that Jesus is approving of me and my work right now, and will in the life to come.

I shouldn't need any other affirmation, I tell myself. But sometimes I do (or think I do). However, I ask God to keep me as balanced as the Apostle Paul: "But by the grace of God I am what I am, and his grace to me was not without effect. No, I worked harder than all of them—yet not I, but the grace of God that was with me" (1 Cor 15:10).

Ultimately, I am not working to get rewards that may be given to me in material terms. I cannot compel myself to do that. But I am working diligently for Jesus every day, for the pleasures I receive now and whatever pleasures I will receive in glory forever. I am very thankful for the teaching of God's word on rewards, and am excited that I will be rewarded. But my primary motivation to love God and my neighbors as myself is to bring deep joy to the heart of God now and forever. If I do that, I will be eternally rewarded by being eternally happy.

One more thought: I love to think about my coming experience before the judgment seat of Christ. This is especially exciting to ponder if this judgment time will involve a time alone with Jesus, as mentioned above. I anticipate this event highly. Yet my excitement has little to do with specific crowns or rewards as such.

The Judged Self: Rewards for Believers

My enthusiasm has to do with being with Jesus—my Redeemer, Lord, Guide, Comforter, Teacher, and Best Friend for well over a half-century. I would not be as enthusiastic if I thought I'd be standing in a throng of billions or trillions waiting for my name to be read and hearing what is in my record. If that's how it will be, however, I know it will be best, because God does only the best.

But I think Christ's judgment of me—and everyone—will be much more personal. After all, he has had a personal relationship with each of his children during their earthly lives, so he knows us very well already. Our first face-to-face meeting, if that's what the judgment will be, should not seem strange at all for those who have known and loved and talked intimately with this beautiful Judge so many, many times before.

There will be no pressure on Jesus to get through everyone's appointment within a certain amount of time. I believe that with God and with us on that great occasion, there will be no sensation of the passing of time. At least, that is my thought and, admittedly, my desire. In any case, I want to see Jesus and commune with him forever. The judgment event will be the beginning of everlasting heavenly joy, awaiting all who look for him and to him daily.

8

The Eternal Self
Believers

WE NOW CONSIDER, FINALLY, the Eternal Self for the people of God. This glorious, culminating phase of existence for every redeemed man, woman, and child will begin just after the great judgment and will never end. It is as certain as—far more certain than—tomorrow's sunrise and the wetness of rain, because it is based on the promises of God, which are grounded in the character of God, the one who is perfect in wisdom, power, and love.

This realm of life—this seventh self for every believer—is, by its very nature, exceedingly beyond what we can imagine. Our minds are stretched far beyond their strongest capabilities to grasp the heavenly physics of space, time, and resurrection life. Nonetheless, we are not without the most important truths God wants us to know, to fill us with hope and encouragement as we continue to travel this earthly path to heavenly glory, one mile at a time, one day at a time.

There is surely much symbolism and figurative language in the relevant biblical texts, but there is also, most assuredly, actual and factual reality behind it. Here are two biblical passages that have thrilled the souls of God's faithful people for nearly two thousand years:

The Eternal Self: Believers

> Then I saw "a new heaven and a new earth," for the first heaven and the first earth had passed away, and there was no longer any sea. I saw the Holy City, the new Jerusalem, coming down out of heaven from God, prepared as a bride beautifully dressed for her husband. And I heard a loud voice from the throne saying, "Look! God's dwelling place is now among the people, and he will dwell with them. They will be his people, and God himself will be with them and be their God. 'He will wipe every tear from their eyes. There will be no more death' or mourning or crying or pain, for the old order of things has passed away." He who was seated on the throne said, "I am making everything new! . . . To the thirsty I will give water without cost from the spring of the water of life. Those who are victorious will inherit all this, and I will be their God and they will be my children." (Rev 21:1–7)

> Then the angel showed me the river of the water of life, as clear as crystal, flowing from the throne of God and of the Lamb down the middle of the great street of the city. On each side of the river stood the tree of life, bearing twelve crops of fruit, yielding its fruit every month. And the leaves of the tree are for the healing of the nations. No longer will there be any curse. The throne of God and of the Lamb will be in the city, and his servants will serve him. They will see his face, and his name will be on their foreheads. There will be no more night. They will not need the light of a lamp or the light of the sun, for the Lord God will give them light. And they will reign for ever and ever. (Rev 22:1–5)

I have not quoted the remaining verses of chapter 21, but recorded as one unit with the above texts, they fill out the single most important account in the Bible concerning heaven and the Eternal Self. The most exciting truths in these scriptures concern both what is *not* in the new heaven and new earth (death, mourning, crying, pain) and—even more—what (who) *is* there (God himself and his people from all the ages). The language is both astonishing and exceedingly tender. "God himself will be with them. . . . He will wipe every tear from their eyes. . . . They will see his face."

How Much May We Speculate?

As just mentioned, there is symbolic language in the biblical accounts of eternal blessedness. For example, because God does not have physical hands, he cannot literally wipe every tear from our eyes. (Unless the divine comforter is Jesus, who, in his resurrected body will physically attend to every crying person in heaven.)

Two questions can be asked to further this line of thought. First, will the New Jerusalem be an actual city, and, if so, will it be made of pure gold, with the great street also made of gold, and each gate made of a single pearl (Rev 21:18, 21)? Second, was this language of gold, pearls, and precious stones, and "the river of the water of life" employed by the Spirit-led, first century writer meant to represent the most valuable earthly things one could imagine at that time and in that place (Rev 1:10–11; 22:16)?

This issue of literal versus symbolic language affects our interpretation not only of the description of our eternal home in Rev 21 and 22, but also of the whole last book of the Bible and large sections of the Bible elsewhere (especially the prophets) that speak of future earthly judgments and earthly blessings, mostly in the final days of human history.

Adding to the difficulty of trying to understand our eternal home in glory is the question of the millennium, a remarkable golden age said to be a thousand years in duration (Rev 20:1–10). Many Bible interpreters say that this period of Christ's rule will occur just after the coming time of great tribulation described in Rev 6–19, and before the final judgment and the eternal state.

I believe that this understanding of the millennium (which may or may not be precisely one thousand years long) is the correct one, although some Bible expositors believe that the millennium is a way of speaking of Christ's spiritual rulership now, from his position at the right hand of the Father. The latter interpreters obviously discern a much heavier use of figurative language in Rev 20 than do the former.

The relevance of the millennial issue in this discussion of the eternal state has to do with substantial Old Testament prophecies

The Eternal Self: Believers

of a glorious future time of righteousness and peace on earth (see, for example, Isa 11–12; 60; Zech 14). Do these predictions of the wolf living peacefully with the lamb, herds of camels covering the land, the ending of sunsets and moon cycles forever, and the Lord being king over the whole earth all refer to a long millennial time for restored Israel and other people on a renewed earth, and before the eternal state? Or do they depict the eternal state itself, or perhaps some combination of the two?

The language of these prophecies is similar to the accounts of the new heaven and new earth in Isa 65:17—66:24 and Rev 21–22. If these prophecies refer to eternity (perhaps, in places, to a prior millennium also), but use time-bound language understandable to the Middle-Easterners at the time of writing, then God's people today have a wealth of additional information about our forever home—substantially more than that in the last book of the Bible.

Even if much of the language is time-bound (the infant playing safely near the cobra's den), the kinds of blessings we will experience, such as peace, justice, and holiness on earth and flourishing for everyone in all areas of life imaginable, can be powerfully encouraging for all who love our Lord and serve him faithfully in this present world of horrendous violence, sin, and suffering. In the end, our God will set everything right.

These matters of biblical interpretation regarding end-times events are beyond the scope of this brief look at our future home in glory. However, I can recommend two fine—though quite different—substantial books on the relevant principles of interpretation as well as just about any other questions you may have about our eternal home. *Heaven*, by Randy Alcorn, and *Probing Heaven*, by John Gilmore, will surely stimulate your mind and soul, as well as your imagination.

Alcorn leans to a more literal understanding of the prophetic language in the Book of Revelation and elsewhere in the Bible (while recognizing some obvious instances of symbolism), whereas Gilmore sees figurative language and symbolism as predominant. Most important, both acknowledge a divinely inspired record of things to come, and both are valuable and fascinating studies of the life awaiting the people of God.

What Will Life in Heaven Be Like?

The way I see things (admittedly, through a glass, darkly, 1 Cor 13:12, KJV), our lives in eternal glory will be, to a great extent, much like what God's people now in the intermediate state (our saved loved ones and all believers of all time) experience, except that there will be more physicality in the eternal state. Two biblical emphases lead me to this tentative conclusion.

First, we will have resurrection bodies, described in 1 Cor 15, especially verses 35–54. While these are said to be *spiritual* bodies, this does not mean that they will be immaterial. We will not be ghost-like creatures, because we will be like Jesus in his resurrection body, and he was a material person who could be touched, and who could eat if he chose to. He is described as the "firstfruits" (the earliest vegetables, grains, or fruits of the season) of a great harvest of God's people—the faithful of all the ages. We will be raised in bodies like the resurrection body of Jesus, even though exact replication of our mortal bodies is not something we can be certain about.

> Christ has indeed been raised from the dead, the firstfruits of those who have fallen asleep. For since death came through a man, the resurrection of the dead comes also through a man. For as in Adam all die, so in Christ all will be made alive. But each in turn: Christ, the firstfruits; then, when he comes, those who belong to him. (1 Cor 15:20–23; see also vss 40–49)

Second, our everlasting home is spoken of as a new heaven and a new earth (Rev 21:1). While the description of this new creation in the last two chapters of Revelation (and in the last two chapters of Isaiah) is undoubtedly thick in symbolism, reflecting the culture and thought patterns of the times, there surely is a

The Eternal Self: Believers

material substratum upon which physical life, activities, and relationships will be enjoyed.

I see no reason why the new Jerusalem, which appears to be in existence even now (Rev 3:12; 21:2-3, 9-10; Heb 12:22-24) cannot be a physical entity of some kind on the new earth, perhaps a massive cube-like structure with a very thick lower wall, yet with gates that are never closed (Rev 21:15-17, 25). This physical world-within-a-world, which would descend from its present location to its permanent home on the approximate region of the old Jerusalem, would then be the capital of the renewed or recreated planet earth and the new heavens, since "the throne of God and of the Lamb" will be there.

The Lamb is, of course, the resurrected and glorified Jesus—the God-man. Because he will be human (and divine, of course) forever, his bodily self will be localized somewhere, seemingly the throne in the New Jerusalem, on the new earth. The wording of the Thirty-Nine Articles of the Church of England, written in 1571, is quite specific: "Christ did truly rise again from death, and took again his body, with flesh, bones, and all things appertaining to the perfection of Man's nature; wherewith he ascended into Heaven, and there sitteth, until he return to judge all Men at the last day."

After the final judgment, heaven will be, for all eternity, based on earth. It seems to me that we will be able to go in and out of its capital city freely, and possibly even explore and live in the new heavens, as God will explain in our instruction packet when we arrive in the eternal kingdom after the judgment. In our glorified, spiritual, touchable bodies, like that of Jesus, we may be able to materialize and dematerialize at will, as Jesus did in the upper room after his resurrection, and with the disciples in the Emmaus Road kitchen (Luke 24:28-43; John 20:19-29; see also Matt 17:1-8, concerning Moses and Elijah on the mount with Jesus).

There will be degrees of reward for each person in glory, which should motivate us now to love God fully and our neighbors as ourselves, in preparation for life as eternal selves, and to bring great joy to the heart of God in our daily activities at present (1 Cor 3:12-15; 2 Cor 5:10; Col 3:23-25; 2 John 8).

Ever Moving On

As the redeemed of the Lord, we will exist as conscious, joyful, embodied selves—probably with all five of our present senses, and maybe even more. We will live in a material universe of some kind throughout eternity: a new heaven and a new earth. I picture trees, rivers, mountains, flowers, and meadows, since God in the beginning created such a world (Eden) for our enjoyment and flourishing.

I truly hope, however, that there will be no awareness of time passing. However, I know that whatever God does with respect to time—seemingly created by him as a condition of the old earth and heaven—will be perfect and delightful. I like to think that each of God's children will be fully in the moment throughout the eternal state, with no distracting awareness of past or future. I also hope, passionately, that there will be no mosquitos, but if there are, I believe they will be like harmless, tiny, beautiful butterflies!

For many years I have asked myself: If I could have only one chapter of the Bible with me for the rest of my life, what chapter would that be? I always reply: Rom 8. There are several powerful themes and sections in this chapter that lead me to this answer, and one of these sections is verses 18–25. Here we read of the new creation—sure to come and never to end.

God's redeemed people will be delivered from the sorrows and sufferings of this present world. In addition, the material creation itself "will be liberated from its bondage to decay, and brought into the freedom and glory of the children of God" (v 21). If we love to gaze upon the beautiful wonders of the earth, oceans, and skies today—in both their immensity and tiniest details—how much more resplendent and glorious will be the colors, shapes, sounds, smells, tastes, and tangible experiences of the new creation: the new heavens and the new earth.

Will we do the things in heaven that we enjoy doing now on earth? We can only speculate, but it seems very likely to me that God—our endlessly creative designer and lavish giver of good and pleasurable things—will bring into being (or equip us to bring into being) all kinds of occupations and activities to delight us in ways unimaginable now.

The Eternal Self: Believers

If a believer really enjoyed quilting on earth, why not assume that God will give such a person that enjoyment in glory, but at an even greater level of satisfaction? The same can be surmised of such pursuits as soccer, hiking, mountain climbing, gardening, woodworking, engineering, reading, learning, conversation (at all levels and on all topics), dancing, guitar playing, baking, chess, oratory, and napping. If these activities won't be in heaven, then God will have even more enjoyable ones for us. We certainly won't need to yearn for any of our former pursuits.

I do hope, however, that I can sit with some special ones—perhaps including James, Esther, Adam, and you—on the bank of a beautiful, shady stream, watching the ducks swim by. If such speculation seems too unspiritual (or even silly) for some folks, we might want to ask them what *they* think we will do in heaven. If we dislike thinking of heaven in concrete ways, and remove such speculation as the above from our idea of heaven, we may be left with little or nothing for which to look forward.

Our everlasting home will be far superior to the Garden of Eden, since there will be no serpent, or even the possibility of sin. There will be no memory of past sins, ours or those of others. We will talk directly with Jesus and his redeemed from all the ages, and quite likely with the angels, since they are personal beings also (Dan 8:15–19; 9:20–23; Luke 1:11–20, 26–38). I can't wait to find out if we will talk directly with the Father and the Holy Spirit also, since they are personal selves just as the Son, as shown in chapters 14–17 of John's gospel. I believe that we will.

Other than being with God forever, one of our supreme delights (referred to in the discussion of the Intermediate Self) will be communing with those special ones (family members and friends) who preceded us in death. The hymnwriter Virgil P. Brock wrote "Beyond the Sunset" in 1936. It has been for many decades one of the most beloved hymns for the people of God:

> Beyond the Sunset, O glad reunion,
> With our dear loved ones who've gone before;
> In that fair homeland, we'll know no parting.
> Beyond the sunset forever more.

Ever Moving On

A wonderful experience I recommend for every reader sometime soon is to read the beautiful words of Jesus at the end of his remarks to each of the seven churches in Rev 2 and 3, concerning those who choose to be true to him. The language is highly symbolic, and follows some severe rebukes, but the glorious realities of which Jesus speaks are a very significant part of the scriptural material on what heaven will be like.

No End of Questions, No End of Blessings

There are a great many questions God's children have asked for centuries concerning what heaven will be like. What will we do? How will we worship God? Will animals (even our earthly pets) be there? Alcorn and Gilmore address these questions and numerous others. Alcorn even asks: Will we drink coffee in heaven? and Will our bodies shine? Gilmore asks, Will there be ownership in heaven? and Will there be humor there? Both ask (as all books on heaven do) about sex in heaven. And Alcorn will encourage many when he writes: "Our new bodies, I expect, will have a natural beauty that won't need cosmetics or touch-ups. As for fat, because God created fat as part of our bodies, we'll surely have some, but in healthy proportion."[1]

Concerning our eternal home, Alcorn discusses arts, entertainment, sports, crafts, technology, new modes of travel, and includes chapters titled as questions: What will we know and learn? What will our daily lives be like? Will heaven ever be boring? He relates:

> An elderly gentleman I led to Christ asked a question of a Christian employee in his care center: "Will we have fun in Heaven?" "Oh, *no*," the woman replied, appearing dismayed that he'd even asked. When he told me this story, I shook my head, because I've heard it so often. . . . [She] instinctively linked fun with sin, and boredom with holiness. But she couldn't be more

---

1. Alcorn, *Heaven*, 289.

The Eternal Self: Believers

wrong. God promises that we'll laugh, rejoice, and experience endless pleasures in Heaven.[2]

Martin Luther said, "If you're not allowed to laugh in heaven, I don't want to go there." John Wesley remarked, "The best is yet to be." Simone Weil declared, "Imaginary evil is romantic and varied; real evil is gloomy, monotonous, barren, boring. Imaginary good is boring; real good is always new, marvelous, intoxicating." And King David wrote, "In Your presence is fullness of joy; at Your right hand are pleasures forevermore" (Ps 16:11, NKJV).

One more passage of the Bible concerning heaven, though seldom recognized as such, is found in the majestic and mysterious epistle to the Hebrews. The human writer was led by the divine author to present a contrast between Mount Sinai and Mount Zion (compare Gal 4:21–31). Mount Sinai (a past, material, earthly reality and experience) represents the strictness and fiery presence of God toward those who attempt to approach him and know him through earthly means alone (Heb 12:18–21). Mount Zion (a present, spiritual reality and experience) represents the graciousness of God toward those who come to him through his merciful plan of redemption in the Savior.

> You have not come to a mountain that can be touched and that is burning with fire. . . . But you have come to Mount Zion, to the city of the living God, the heavenly Jerusalem. You have come to thousands upon thousands of angels in joyful assembly, to the church of the firstborn, whose names are written in heaven. You have come to God, the Judge of all, to the spirits of the righteous made perfect, to Jesus the mediator of a new covenant. . . . Therefore . . . let us be thankful, and so worship God acceptably with reverence and awe, for our God is a consuming fire. (Heb 12:18–29)

These words speak of our heavenly experience on two levels: first, what believers on earth experience now (spiritually) through Jesus our heavenly high priest, having access to God's presence through prayer and communion with other believers (Heb

---

2. Alcorn, *Heaven*, 410–11.

4:14–16; 10:19–25); and second, what believers in glory experience now (materially) in the heavenly Jerusalem, presently existing in heaven (Heb 11:10, 16; 13:14), awaiting its relocation on the new earth (Isa 65:17–18; Rev 21:1–2, 10).

Can We Be Too Heavenly Minded?

It has been said often that if one becomes too heavenly minded they will be of no earthly good. I and millions of others affirm, however, that the more heavenly minded a person becomes, the more earthly good they can accomplish. This has been demonstrated over the centuries by devout people of God in every region on earth, in every culture and racial group, and in every occupation and sphere of service for God and humanity.

I have read many excellent biographies and autobiographies of men and women who were truly heavenly minded and, because of that, were significant agents for earthly good as well as spiritual, eternal benefit for large numbers. The Christian missionary movements of recent centuries, for example, have resulted in a great many highly beneficial hospitals, institutions of learning, linguistic and translation societies, agencies for agricultural and water-related development, and relief organizations funded and staffed by an abundance of heavenly minded givers, volunteers, and career workers who love what they do.

> Then the King will say to those on his right, "Come, you who are blessed by my Father; take your inheritance, the kingdom prepared for you since the creation of the world. For I was hungry and you gave me something to eat, I was thirsty and you gave me something to drink, I was a stranger and you invited me in, I needed clothes and you clothed me, I was sick and you looked after me, I was in prison and you came to visit me." (Matt 25:34–36)

My favorite poem (quoted here as prose) was written by Robert Murray M'Cheyne of Scotland (1813–43). M'Cheyne was a servant of God who influenced me toward godly living more than any other person during the first twenty years of my Christian life.

The Eternal Self: Believers

The poem, penned in 1837, is titled "When This Passing World Is Done." I include three of the stanzas to close this discussion of believers' eternal selves. I can think of no more overwhelming words on the topic of heaven, or on any other topic.

> When this passing world is done, When has sunk yon glaring sun;
>
> When we stand with Christ in glory, Looking o'er life's finished story;
>
> Then, Lord, shall I fully know, Not till then, how much I owe.
>
> When I stand before the throne, Dressed in beauty not my own;
>
> When I see thee as thou art, Love thee with unsinning heart;
>
> Then, Lord, shall I fully know, Not till then, how much I owe.
>
> Chosen not for good in me, Wakened up from wrath to flee;
>
> Hidden in the Savior's side, By the Spirit sanctified;
>
> Teach me, Lord, on earth to show, By my love, how much I owe.[3]

---

3. Bonar, *M'Cheyne*, 636–37.

9

Dangers, Conclusions, and Hope

IN THIS INCREDIBLE JOURNEY of the seven selves we have been moving on from the womb to life well beyond the grave. We have come to see that almost all of our life will be lived after we die. Except for the tiny speck of existence within our mother's body, and the somewhat longer but still tiny moment of existence while we walk through this world, our journey of life is really a journey of the afterlife.

Our earthly life is but a blip on God's radar screen—"a mist that appears for a little while and then vanishes" (Jas 4:14). However, what we do in this life determines what we will do for all eternity. We must give our utmost attention, then, to the porch of our future home, and what happens on this porch as we move, step by step, toward the front door.

Once we go through the door of death, we will enter a mysterious realm entirely different from anything we have ever known or imagined. And, once on the other side, we will understand how the journey of our earthly life has fixed the course of our journey to come. We will no longer be active participants in spiritual decision-making, still charting our own autonomous course, but will follow the way determined by God for everyone who has ever lived.

Dangers, Conclusions, and Hope

In this final chapter, because of the crucial place God gives to our life on earth, it seems best to think once again about our journey over the highway of time, beginning with the dangers along the way. We will then draw some conclusions about our adventure of ideas and actions, and then focus with great delight on the hope that keeps us moving on, stepping ever closer to the door—the entrance to the great beyond.

Dangers Along the Way

As mentioned earlier, the book *Pilgrim's Progress* has guided and encouraged millions throughout the centuries to seek the One who alone has the answers to life's biggest questions. Many of these seekers have come to know and follow the Lord Jesus Christ, who referred to himself as "the way and the truth and the life" (John 14:6).

Along the pathway to the Celestial City, the New Jerusalem, our pilgrim encountered "many dangers, toils, and snares." Some of these were terrible places such as Doubting Castle, the Hill Called Error, the Slough of Despond, and the Valley of the Shadow of Death.

So it is today. Everyone who sets out to find the meaning of life and lasting peace, joy, and love, will encounter deep pits, mountain-sized blockades, and highly attractive diversions off the main highway. Some travelers are severely tempted to turn back because the way ahead appears too difficult, and because a return to the former life is at least familiar, and old friends and activities sometimes call enticingly.

Listed below are twelve of the greatest dangers along the highway to the Celestial City. (There are plenty more.) Whether you are a Christian or an enquirer—wherever you are along the path of life—you have quite likely faced some or all of these dangers. If not, you will, so I present these snares to alert you, and remind myself, of some perils to avoid. "The highway of the upright avoids evil" (Prov 16:17).

While you are walking along, and see a signpost and arrow pointing to one of the following danger areas, step guardedly but firmly past it without panic, with a steady, straight-ahead gaze on the road before you. You may even catch a glimpse, from time to time, of the Celestial City shining brilliantly on the horizon. "Take note of the highway, the road that you take" (Jer 31:24).

The travel brochure below describes each roadside attraction where one may stay as long as one chooses, or return to a previous attraction as often as one wishes. They are all under the same management: His Infernal Majesty, the vicious and relentless enemy of our souls. I must confess that I added to the satanic travel brochure, for each adventure, an "ambience" piece and some highly pertinent Bible verses, even though the management of these popular tourist sites will definitely not appreciate my additions.

Do Come Inn: Twelve Superfine Locations Just for You

Hotel Haughty. (Ambience: Pride.) Here one may sit, stand, strut, or sniff, superior to all else. Face pride, place pride, grace pride, and pride of intellect, opinion, and the absolute right to choose for oneself rule unquestioned. This was our original location, and it remains the foundation and core of all that we strive for at "Do Come Inn." (Prov 16:18; 1 Pet 5:5; Isa 57:15)

Palace of Delights. (Ambience: Pleasure Seeking.) Here one may indulge all sensual and surreal cravings without limit. Exotic foods and drink, sexual experiences, and drugs of every kind, along with assorted arts and entertainment, seduce and grip one tightly. (Luke 8:14; Eph 4:19; Col 3:5)

Hall of Mirrors. (Ambience: People Pleasing.) Here one may enjoy the perfecting of their appearance and persona, and receive the adulation of others who do likewise. Friends gather often to exchange compliments and praise, especially for their many virtues, feelings of compassion and justice, and opinions held in common. (Luke 6:26; Jude 16; 1 Tim 4:8)

Dangers, Conclusions, and Hope

City of Lights. (Ambience: Materialism.) Here one may try out and come to possess all manner of physical things designed to make life easier and more fun. That which cannot be worn, touched, or used for one's material benefit—this includes serious thought—is not highly regarded. (Matt 19:24; Luke 12:15; 1 Tim 6:10)

The Nursery. (Ambience: Emotionalism.) Here one may abandon the irritation of logic and reason and express feelings without restraint. Shouting, screaming, silliness, and hysteria take the place of boring discussion and respectful debate. For those who come here, everything is either-or rather than both-and. A vibrant spirit of lawlessness pervades the facilities. (Prov 10:11; 26:4; Eccl 9:17)

Temple of the Exalted Self. (Ambience: Religious Comfort.) Here one may do church and churchy activities in the finest facilities anywhere; we have terrific preachers, teachers, and musicians. In one of our many exotic cafes you may enjoy warm fellowship with those who believe that happiness in this life is the greatest good. Instead of God, God, God, the focus is on you, you, you—your gratification, your success, and your destiny, all without the old rugged cross. (Isa 58:13–14; Jer 10:21; Luke 9:23)

Scoffer's Cove. (Ambience: Unbelief.) Here one may freely express disdain and scorn toward all authorities and traditions, especially biblically based Christian teachings. While doubters and questioners are welcome, if they are open to grow, scoffers and revilers are especially at home here. (John 8:43–47; 2 Thess 2:10–12; Jude 17–21)

The Big Tent. (Ambience: Intolerance toward Intolerance.) Here, adjacent to Scoffer's Cove and Temple of the Exalted Self, one may finally cast off the shackles of religious dogma and doctrine, and explore and embrace whatever thoughts and practices one chooses, with little or no interference from deeply personal prayer, serious study, or consistency of ideas. With the motto, "Doctrine divides, Love unites," the emphasis is on the certainty and superiority of (almost all) uncertainty. Two things, however, are certain here: (1) the rightness of the lack of tolerance toward those (such as conservative Christians) who are not always affirming (that is, tolerant of Big Tent beliefs and practices) toward others; and (2) the great importance of Big Tent conformity by embracing the exciting differences of all whose personal lifestyles and forceful opinions are refreshingly bizarre, because people are basically good and all but a few truly wretched individuals are going to heaven. One special feature: a scrumptious buffet table, loaded with exotic goodies beyond imagination, where one may create their own god or gods, and their own religion. (Acts 17:22–23; 2 Pet 2:1–3; 1 Tim 4:16)

Sofa World. (Ambience: Laziness.) Here one may loaf endlessly on the plushest beds and furniture, crawling from one piece to another when one can muster the energy. Whether one's tendency is toward physical sloth, mental indolence, or spiritual laziness, there are no reprimands here. (Prov 6:6–11; 26:14–16; 2 Thess 3:10–13; Eccl 4:5)

Care Less Castle. (Ambience: Lovelessness.) Here one may find freedom from all pressures to care deeply about others. If one feels so inclined, one may like those who like them, and even help them, but intense expressions of selflessness, costly compassion, and sacrificial giving are not permitted, since these may disturb the other guests. (1 Tim 6:18–19; 1 John 3:17–18; Jude 22–23)

Bitterland. (Ambience: Unresolved Anger.) Here one may clutch, defend, and cherish resentments of every kind, whether against parents, school officials, other authority figures, spouses, former friends and lovers, former employers, or God. In particular, those who refuse to absolve God of what he has allowed or still allows of terrible suffering in their personal lives and throughout the world will find many to commiserate with here—one of our favorite attractions (Eph 4:26–27, 31; Heb 12:14–15; Lam 3:32–33)

House of Woe. (Ambience: Discouragement.) Here one may shuffle about, cry in a corner, or just sit and feel sad

Dangers, Conclusions, and Hope

over their life circumstances, major disappointments, and lack of love and/or recognition. Some victims dwell here for a very large portion of their journey, returning often when life gets too hard. Among many who want to be faithful Christians, but are not able, this is the most popular of our attractions. Some even die here, within just a few miles of the Celestial City. (Ps 42:3–5; Heb 10:35–36; 2 Thess 2:16–17)

Having just read through the above travel brochure, I feel sad, sick, and angry. You may have similar feelings, and more. I feel a sense of revulsion toward the evil mind and soul of the enemy, and its subtle—and not so subtle—temptation schemes. I recall the biblical warning against those who call evil good and good evil (Isa 5:20). I am determined, therefore, to influence readers and everyone else I can from being pulled toward any of these glamorous diversions along the path of life.

For a time I wondered if I should leave out the travel brochure. Since I am nearing the end of the book, and since the brochure follows right after the uplifting discussion of the new heavens and new earth, I wondered if such a negative piece in this final chapter would leave the reader more downcast than upbeat.

After some thought, I decided to include the roadside attractions. I doubt that serious Christians will be offended by the sarcasm. They will instead, I believe, see the need for these warnings. Jesus, Paul, Elijah, and the God of Isaiah provide ample justification for the use of sarcasm and insulting language when appropriate (1 Kgs 18:27; Isa 44:12–20; 65:2–5; John 8:44; 1 Cor 1:25; Phil 3:2; and perhaps most notably, Gal 5:12, concerning circumcision).

Conclusions

Who are you? Who am I? Who are we becoming? I have written this brief, introductory excursion through the six or seven selves of every person's existence to serve as a biblically based guide to thinking about life: past, present, and future. Unless we responsible selves enter and experience the In-Christ Self, by responding personally and affirmatively to God's gracious invitation and command to receive his forgiveness and lordship during our earthly lives, we will experience only six selves: the Initial Self, the Independent Self, the Intermediate Self, the Resurrected Self, the Judged Self, and the Eternal Self.

It should be startling for us to realize that almost all of our existence takes place after our physical death. Bruce Wilkinson writes and teaches about the dot and the line. He diagrams this concept very simply by putting a dot near the left margin of a page, and to its right, extending to the other margin, he draws a straight line with an arrow at the end. The dot stands for one's life here on earth, somewhere around seventy or eighty years for most people. The line with the arrow (showing that the line never ends) depicts one's life in eternity, forever. As Jesus taught, what happens inside the little dot determines everything that happens on the line.

> Whenever audiences grasp this mental picture, their reactions are immediate and intense. They say things like, "If this is true, it changes everything for me!" Or "I can't believe I've prepared for my children's future and my old age without giving a thought to my *real* future!" One man said to me, "I've always thought about finishing well, but it turns out that death is just the starting gate!"[1]

The brevity and uncertainty of life is a consistent theme of scripture, as seen in the verses here.

> Show me, LORD, my life's end and the number of my days; let me know how fleeting my life is. You have made my days a mere handbreadth; the span of my years is as nothing before you. Everyone is but a breath, even those who seem secure. (Ps 39:4–5)

> LORD, what are human beings that you care for them, mere mortals that you think of them? They are like a breath; their days are like a fleeting shadow. (Ps 144:3–4)

> Stop trusting in mere humans, who have but a breath in their nostrils. (Isa 2:22)

---

1. Wilkinson, *Life God Rewards*, 28–29.

Dangers, Conclusions, and Hope

Why, you do not even know what will happen tomorrow. What is your life? You are a mist that appears for a little while and then vanishes. (Jas 4:14)

Allow me to make a final, fervent plea, from my deepest inner self, to every reader, whether you are young, middle aged, or in your later years. If you are not certain, with the full assurance God longs to give you (Rom 8:16; 2 Tim 1:12) concerning your identity as a born-again child of God, and concerning your everlasting destiny, receive him now, without one more day of hesitation. You may not live to see tomorrow.

Even if you made a decision for Jesus Christ some time ago, and lived what seemed to be a Christian life for years, yet fell away from your belief and trust in God, you cannot expect (even subconsciously in some distorted sense) that your earlier decision and way of life will somehow benefit you when you stand before the God you now say you no longer believe in.

I have rarely been more startled by someone's testimony of losing their faith than I have been since reading the remarkably honest and remarkably chilling words of Bart Ehrman, a former evangelical "devout and committed Christian" (his words) who is a New Testament scholar held in high regard by non-conservative scholars in his field.

> When I fell away from my faith—not just in the Bible as God's inspired word, but in Christ as the only way of salvation, and eventually from the view that Christ was himself divine, and beyond that from the view that there is an all-powerful God in charge of this world—I still wondered, deep down inside: could I have been right after all? What if I was right then but wrong now? Will I burn in hell forever? The fear of death gripped me for years, and there are still moments when I wake up at night in a cold sweat.[2]

C. S. Lewis, in the final words of his classic work, *Mere Christianity*, expresses my burden and my plea far more powerfully than anyone I am familiar with, with the exception of Jesus:

---

2. Quoted in Alcorn, *If God Is Good*, 322.

Ever Moving On

> Give up yourself, and you will find your real self. Lose your life and you will save it. Submit to death, death of your ambitions and favorite wishes every day and death of your whole body in the end: submit with every fiber of your being, and you will find eternal life. Keep back nothing. Nothing that you have not given away will ever be really yours. Nothing in you that has not died will ever be raised from the dead. Look for yourself, and you will find in the long run only hatred, loneliness, despair, rage, ruin, and decay. But look for Christ and you will find Him, and with Him everything else thrown in.[3]

To you who have yielded decisively to God through trust in Christ, with no reliance on your good works to influence God in your favor (Eph 2:8–9; Titus 3:4–5), I exhort you (as I daily exhort myself) to live fully as the In-Christ Self God has said you are positionally and has made you to be actually, to love him wholly and your neighbors as yourself. My deepest desire, which I offer to you as well, is to live the rest of my days here on earth increasing in spiritual maturity, godliness, wisdom, helpfulness to others, and in intimacy with God: Father, Son, and Holy Spirit.

This will not happen without our consistently meditating (not just reading quickly, to say we did something) in the scriptures daily, if only one or two verses (unless health or other crises prevent), frequent interactions, worship experiences, and gatherings for learning and encouragement with like-minded people of God, reading some words from those (alive or in glory) who have written profoundly of the great themes of our Christian faith, and continually speaking with our Lord about everything throughout the day, as well as in quiet, extended times alone with him, with a grateful heart that leads to unselfish service for those in need.

God's children have a truly amazing future, full of his infinite grace and glory. It is toward this future that we are ever moving on. "For now we see only a reflection as in a mirror; then we shall see face to face. Now I know in part; then I shall know fully, even as I am fully known" (1 Cor 13:12).

---

3. Lewis, *Mere Christianity*, 190.

Dangers, Conclusions, and Hope

Hope

As Pilgrim (whose name was Christian) progressed along the difficult road to the New Jerusalem, all was not discouragement, fearfulness, or gloom. He came across numerous individuals who helped and motivated him greatly in his attempt to stay true to his Savior and Lord. Some of these were Faithful, Evangelist, Piety, and a man named Hopeful.

The last became Christian's brotherly covenant partner, and his devoted traveling companion, until the end of their journey to the Celestial City. In my little edition (a somewhat ragged paperback I purchased for 75 cents over fifty years ago), this last phase of their pilgrimage covers over half of Christian's life with a beloved and loyal friend. How richly blessed we would all be to have such a hope-full partner with whom to move through life with.

When Christian met Jesus at Calvary, and the burden of his sin fell from his back, he rose from the ground at the foot of the cross, looked into the eyes of his Redeemer, and felt—among other sensations—hope. Yes, he experienced peace, freedom, joy, love, trust, forgiveness, cleanliness, and many other sensations. But I am convinced he also experienced hope. He may not have thought about the word at that time, just as I did not at the time of my coming to the cross at the age of nineteen. But both Christian and I definitely had a sensation of hope.

The word hope is used about 180 times in the Bible. God obviously considers hope to be necessary—not optional—in the lives of people. The most common meaning for the English noun "hope," according to Webster's, is "a feeling that what is wanted will happen; desire accompanied by expectation." A person might say, "I am filled with hope." The verb may also have this optimistic note: "I hope it's a sunny day tomorrow." Sometimes, however, hope has a pessimistic tone, or at least a hesitation about whether the outcome will be good: "I hope this dentist appointment doesn't hurt too much."

The *biblical* idea of hope is overwhelmingly one of confident optimism, trusting in the God who can do all things. Such confidence is in the character, past actions, fulfilled and future prophecies, and experienced promises of God, not in circumstances or luck, as in the case of most secular uses of the word.

Listed below are some of the many scripture texts concerning hope, enabling us to get some idea of what *biblical* hope is, in contrast with the rather feeble connotations commonly associated with hope.

> Though he slay me, yet will I hope in him.... (Job 13:15)

> No one who hopes in you will ever be put to shame.... (Ps 25:3)

> Guide me in your truth and teach me, for you are God my Savior, and my hope is in you all day long. (Ps 25:5)

> As for me, I will always have hope; I will praise you more and more. (Ps 71:14)

> Even youths grow tired and weary, and young men stumble and fall; but those who hope in the LORD will renew their strength. (Isa 40:30–31)

> The LORD is good to those whose hope is in him, to the one who seeks him; it is good to wait quietly for the salvation of the LORD. (Lam 3:25–26)

> And we boast in the hope of the glory of God. Not only so, but we also glory in our sufferings, because we know that suffering produces perseverance; perseverance, character; and character, hope. And hope does not put us to shame, because God's love has been poured out into our hearts through the Holy Spirit, who has been given to us. (Rom 5:2–5)

> Be joyful in hope, patient in affliction, faithful in prayer. (Rom 12:12)

> For everything that was written in the past was written to teach us, so that through the endurance taught in the Scriptures and the encouragement they provide we might have hope. (Rom 15:4)

Dangers, Conclusions, and Hope

May the God of hope fill you with all joy and peace as you trust in him, so that you may overflow with hope by the power of the Holy Spirit. (Rom 15:13)

[Love] always protects, always trusts, always hopes, always perseveres. (1 Cor 13:7)

And now these three remain: faith, hope and love. But the greatest of these is love. (1 Cor 13:13)

If only for this life we have hope in Christ, we are of all people most to be pitied. (1 Cor 15:19)

May our Lord Jesus Christ himself and God our Father, who loved us and by his grace gave us eternal encouragement and good hope, encourage your hearts and strengthen you in every good deed and word. (2 Thess 2:16-17)

For the grace of God has appeared that offers salvation to all people. It teaches us . . . while we wait for the blessed hope—the appearing of the glory of the great God and Savior, Jesus Christ. . . . (Titus 2:11-13)

We have this hope as an anchor for the soul, firm and secure. (Heb 6:19)

Let us hold unswervingly to the hope we profess, for he who promised is faithful. (Heb 10:23)

Now faith is confidence in what we hope for and assurance about what we do not see. (Heb 11:1)

Always be prepared to give an answer to everyone who asks you to give the reason for the hope that you have. (1 Pet 3:15)

The Nature of Biblical Hope

From a careful reading of these and similar scriptures we can see something of the biblical meaning of this robust little word. There are several key facets of biblical hope for believers that stand out: (1) hope is closely associated with joy; (2) hope anticipates a positive future with God in control; (3) hope fosters encouragement and endurance in the present; (4) hope looks to the coming fulfillment (telos, purpose, culmination, consummation) of God's program for the old creation and the full inauguration of his kingdom throughout the new creation; (5) hope is an indispensable, God-given emotional component of our daily Christian walk and service in this world.

Biblical hope is entwined with both future events and present realities. This dual confidence ought to bolster every believer regularly. New Testament scholar N. T. Wright, however, offers a sobering comment in this regard. "Most people, in my experience—including many Christians—don't know what the ultimate Christian hope really is. Most people—again, sadly, including many Christians—don't expect Christians to have much to say about hope within the present world. Most people don't imagine that these two could have anything to do with each other."[4] These two horizons, however, are inseparably connected, and each is based on the foundational *biblical* concept of hope. Here, my personal experience may help to illustrate this relationship.

Never in my life have I understood hope as I do now, as I write this book. Over the decades I preached on some of the major biblical texts on hope, such as those quoted above, because I was preaching through the Bible book or passage where such texts was found. But my thoughts and words, although (I trust) led by the Spirit, never rang a bell within me nor gripped me as they do now.

In April 2020, the most difficult month of my life ever regarding physical pain, I was skimming through the TV channels. I paused for a few moments when I heard a Christian teacher (Joyce Meyer) briefly emphasizing hope. God used her few words to ignite something within me that was gripping, eye-opening, and very encouraging. She stressed how absolutely vital hope was in the life of a Christian, *in every stage and experience of life*. No one can make it through life without sustained hope. That's really all I heard her say, but it stayed with me, and grew.

---

4. Wright, *Surprised by Hope*, xi.

Dangers, Conclusions, and Hope

Before this, I had a somewhat uneasy relationship with the word hope, because I considered it to be a more emotional term for faith, and I was uncomfortable with emotions (feelings) as a major part of Christian living. I thought from time to time of the little diagram from evangelist Bill Bright depicting three cars in a train, in this order: facts, faith, feelings. Our salvation and Christian life are based solidly on (and pulled by) the engine: facts—the incarnation, teachings, miracles, crucifixion, resurrection, and ascension of Jesus Christ.

We rest our faith (the passenger car following the engine) on these certain facts. We move through life with a rock-solid trust in Christ and in the facts about him that ground our convictions and actions. The third car is the caboose. This car carries our feelings, which can vary wildly, sometimes buoying us up while at other times throwing us to the ground. These should not be relied on for guidance or assurance from God. Feelings will vary—often quite a lot—with circumstances, and are not reliable. We must ground our faith—our beliefs, words, and behaviors—on the facts of the gospel, not on our feelings.

This train diagram contains valuable and essential truth. It has undoubtedly helped millions, including me, through the storms of life. I am very grateful for the key lessons taught hereby. But I moved through the years, as stated above, with a hesitancy about emotions having much of a part in my life. I was grounded in the facts of scripture, and my confidence was in the truth I had come to know and believe.

I was never quite certain what to do with the hope in 1 Cor 13:13: "And now these three remain: faith, hope and love. But the greatest of these is love." Yet I preached on this verse and the surrounding verses, and I presented this text as God's threefold truth.

Now I am much clearer about the text and the concepts. Faith is primarily belief (trust and assurance) in God. It has to do fundamentally with ideas and truths. But it is not only cognitive; it is volitional—the mind informing the will. Love is primarily action, propelled by faith and hope. It may or may not have a significant emotional element. Hope is primarily feeling—deep emotion (affection) grounded in the truths of faith that leads to the actions of love.

Faith believes and trusts—rooted in the facts: the past actions, words, and promises of God. It moves out to follow God no matter what the obstacles, as the great stalwarts of faith in Heb 11 are said to have done. Abraham, Sarah, Moses, and Rahab all obeyed God "by faith." The majestic Epistle to the Romans, declaring our justification by faith as no other, begins and ends with "the obedience that comes from faith" (1:5; 16:26).

Hope believes and feels, stimulated by faith and bolstered by a deep, inner joy and confidence from God that looks to future victory (both near and distant) according to God's timing and wisdom. Even though the primary focus of hope is the future, it is very much for today, just as are faith and love. No Christian should begin his or her day without a good dose of hope.

Love, "the greatest of these," is superior because when it sees a need and knows it should help, it goes to work now, in the present, to seek the highest honor of God and the greatest good of others, when good is defined according to the teachings of the scriptures: godliness, mercy, justice, peace, housing, food, employment, clothing, warm smiles, looks and touch as appropriate, compassionate care for the weak and hurting, and instruction in the ways of God and the numerous skills (including social ones) for living life wisely. Godly love is based solidly on godly faith and godly hope, and emerges continually from them.

God, Hope, and Emotion

As well as being faith-filled and love-filled children of God, we can be and must be hope-filled, more than ever in these dark days. Our God is a God of hope, and we are created in his image to be a people of hope. God is an emotional (feeling, affective) God, as well as a cognitive (thinking) God and a volitional (choosing) God. We too, therefore, are blessed to be emotional beings.

Some theologians and philosophers of religion have denied the emotional side of God, because they say this would make God

Dangers, Conclusions, and Hope

a changeable God, as when, for example, he would be *more* angry or *more* joyful than at another time. He would not be absolutely immutable, as they claim he is.

A wide and deep reading of the Bible, however, dispels such a rigid philosophical concept. "In all their distress, he too was distressed" (Isa 63:9). This verse uses the same Hebrew word of God as of the Israelites, meaning affliction, suffering, and anguish.

> Is not Ephraim [Israel] my dear son, the child in whom I delight? Though I often speak against him, I still remember him. Therefore my heart yearns for him; I have great compassion for him, declares the LORD. (Jer 31:20)

> When Israel was a child, I loved him, and out of Egypt I called my son. But the more they were called, the more they went away from me. . . . [They] refuse to repent. . . . [So] a sword will flash in their cities; it will devour their false prophets and put an end to their plans. . . . [Yet], how can I give you up, Ephraim? . . . My heart is changed within me; all my compassion is aroused. I will not carry out my fierce anger, nor will I devastate Ephraim again. (Hos 11:1-9)

God feels anger, and sometimes acts upon it. God feels compassion, and sometimes acts upon it. God also feels hope, because he alone knows the what and why of his kingdom program. He always acts for the good of those who come to him in humility and weakness, as a little child. Sometimes, in hope, he must punish people for their good (both temporal and eternal good) to draw them to himself. Because we have such a God of hope we can be a people of deep hope and its partners: deep faith, deep love, deep peace, and deep joy.

Hope is a hearty cognitive and emotional confidence and way of life based on God's past, present, and future triumphs over his enemies, and our assured triumphs with him now and forever. "May the God of hope fill you with all joy and peace as you trust in him, so that you may overflow with hope by the power of the Holy Spirit" (Rom 15:13). "But now I am coming to Thee," said Jesus to his Father, "and I speak these words while I am in the world, in order that they may have my gladness within them filling their hearts" (John 17:13, Weymouth).

God is interested in the cognitive, affective, and volitional aspects of our lives: faith, hope, and love. He is also highly concerned about the relational and social dimensions of our lives: how we live personally before and with him and our neighbors in the realms of our words, thoughts, and deeds.

Returning to the train diagram, but with a somewhat different configuration of my own, we may think of a Christian as a train pulled by a powerful facts-faith lead car, followed by a work-horse main car of faithful living and serving, trailed by a lowly caboose of emotions—except that, as we've seen, this caboose is not so lowly. It is essential, as long as it is not allowed to wag the train.

A Christian writer from my teen years, Fulton Oursler, said that many people crucify themselves between two thieves: regret over the past and fear of the future. Yet, whether believer or nonbeliever, no one needs to be crucified by either of these thieves. Both the lost and the redeemed may put their hope in the one crucified on the middle cross.

I wish I had seen the full-orbed meaning of biblical hope many years ago as I see it now. On May 4, 2020, while lying on my hospital bed at four o'clock in the morning, several days after major surgery, so very weary of lying there, I clicked on the TV and turned to a program of instrumental music called Soundscapes. Each panel was a nature scene with a saying designed to give hope. One from Oliver Wendell Holmes struck me, and I wrote down the basic idea: Once you have been exposed to a new idea, your mind is never able to return to its former way of thinking. My new, God-given insight on hope has changed my way of thinking, feeling, and being. I am grateful.

Thanksgiving for Grace and Hope

Flowing from gratitude (concerning hope and emotion) is a need to emphasize and cultivate one vital task—and joy—of every Christian: thanksgiving. Every serious believer knows almost instinctively the rightness and radiance of this remarkable responsibility. It is "the song of the soul set free." Second only to the adoration (worship) of God, thanksgiving is our most vital and joyful obligation and privilege daily, even many times a day. Whereas adoration is praising God for who he is in himself, thanksgiving is praising God for what he has said or done on our behalf, and what he will yet say and do for us and the entire creation.

This being so, how can we possibly express thanks to God without emotion, not to mention adoring him without emotion? Yet, for most of my life, while I have been a thankful person, my expressions of gratitude were, I think, mostly cognitive. I know I *felt* what I was saying, but I was mostly uttering "Thank you, God" out of a full head of glorious biblical truths. Now I still do this, but it is with a full heart as well.

It is much richer and more pleasurable (and more delightful to God) to offer thanks (as well as worship) out of both head and heart—thinking and feeling overwhelmed with God, and telling him the why's and what's of my thanks in specific details, from his word and from my life experiences.

To me, the most important word in the Bible, other than the names of God, is *grace*: God's pure, unearned gifts of love to us through Christ in saving us from destruction (in both this life and the next), and strengthening us daily, inwardly and outwardly, as we live and serve for his glory and the good of others. As recipients of God's daily grace, our proper response must be daily gratitude. Grace is God's attitude and action toward us, and gratitude is our attitude and action toward God and others in response.

Grace and gratitude may be thought of as two sides of one coin—a coin we might call, biblically, *union with Christ*. We are one with him and he with us. In light of such an intimate In-Christ life, how can we live without regularly feeling, to some extent, God's presence, promises, and provisions? This life of hope, with all that has been said above, is the reason so many of God's faithful people walk about with a genuine and grateful contentment—even a smile from deep within—on their faces.

Ever Moving On

Before leaving the topic of hope in the Christian life, a very important caution is necessary. If you, for example, express hope that you will be hired for that job you want, or that you will marry that person you long for, or that you or a loved one will be healed of a chronic disease, you need to be careful. I have been disappointed in matters such as these (not the marriage part), and I suspect some of you have been as well.

At this point we understandably ask, if hope is not only emotional, but grounded in the rock-solid facts of our faith, why does God allow these disappointments? If we have a solid basis for being people of hope, why then are our hopes sometimes left unfulfilled?

My reply, incomplete for sure, is that biblical hope has to do primarily with the overall program of God for the world, and only secondarily with the specifics of our individual lives. A re-reading of the scripture texts on hope quoted earlier will, I believe, confirm the validity of this observation. We are hopeful people because God is in control of this world and its future. We can be assured—cognitively and emotionally—that we are united with our Lord and his kingdom program forever.

The details of our lives, while very important to God, are not to be the major focus of our hope as the Bible uses the word. Rather, such hope is meant to function as "an anchor for the soul" (Heb 6:19).

When we anticipate something we greatly desire, as Paul longed to visit the believers at Rome (Rom 1:8–15), we must place our hopes and dreams in the hands of the God of all grace (1 Pet 5:10), confident that he alone knows and does what is best for his children in the light of eternity. If our initial hope concerning a certain earthly matter is not fulfilled, our longer-lasting and deeper hope, as members of God's kingdom, and participants in his majestic program through the ages, should not be shattered or diminished. We will sometimes feel sadness, perhaps great sadness, but we return to the assurance that our Lord does all things well, and he continues to infuse us with true hope until the day we see him face to face. "As for God, His way is perfect . . . and

Dangers, Conclusions, and Hope

[He] makes my way perfect" (Ps 18:30, 32, NKJV).[5] This is why we really can give thanks *for* everything and *in* everything (Eph 5:20; 1 Thess 5:18).

Closing Words

As we bring this little book to a close, I trust that every pilgrim reader has been informed, warned, encouraged, and bolstered emotionally and volitionally in our shared journey to the Celestial City.

We are all moving on, from the womb to a fascinating life beyond the grave. Almost all of our life, as we have seen, takes place after our death—after we step from the small porch of earthly life through the wide gates of John Bunyan's Beulah Land. "No longer will they call you Deserted, or name your land Desolate. But you will be called Hephzibah ['my delight is in her'], and your land Beulah ['married']; for the Lord will take delight in you, and your land will be married" (Isa 62:4).

God's relationships with his wayward, lonely, hurting people, including you and me at times, will finally and fully be restored forever, all because of Calvary. At the conclusion (and new beginning) of our journey we will say, not only with head knowledge but also by experience and with deep feeling, "the path of the righteous is like the morning sun, shining ever brighter till the full light of day" (Prov 4:18).

Until then, when our eyes will finally behold the City, we move forward, in hope, triumphantly and humbly, with this our

---

5. The twin problems of evil (the root) and suffering (the fruit), which produce undoubtedly the most serious and widespread set of objections to the orthodox Christian teaching advocating the existence of a supremely good God who is also an all-powerful God, are addressed very helpfully and fully (512 pages) in Alcorn's *If God Is Good*. In addition, much of Strobel's *Case for Faith* is devoted to the issues of evil and suffering, as is chapter one of Blomberg, *Can We Still Believe in God?* Finally, Carson, *How Long, O Lord?*, is a serious, valuable work written especially for believers, mostly as a book of "preventative medicine" to help God's children think through highly important matters before they may have to face even worse sufferings than they may have already endured.

banner out in front: "For this God is our God for ever and ever; he will be our guide even to the end" (Ps 48:14).

Appendix

My Credo

A Message to Those I Care About Most, Concerning the Things that Matter Most

THE PURPOSE. BECAUSE YOU are reading this piece, you are one of those I care about most. This may sound strange because I may barely know you, or may never have met you. But anyone who sees this title, and starts reading this message, is someone I care very much about. Those who are willing to consider the things that matter most are a special group of people.

There is no flattery here. Anyone who thinks of what matters most—even though they may not be clear about what all this term implies—is a searcher after truth and the meaning of life. This world can be a confusing place, filled with both beauty and ugliness, good and evil, truth and lies. I am writing here because, by God's grace, I have found some answers to the biggest questions of life, and cannot hold back from sharing what I believe strongly to be true. (The word "credo" is Latin for "I believe." In English it is used as a noun meaning a statement of beliefs or convictions, as I use it here.)

The Readers. Originally I intended to write this to my five grandchildren, because of my deep love for them and my special interest

Appendix

in them. They are now young adults and have good minds and hearts. Since I am now in my seventies and have poor health, I have a burning desire to express briefly to them what God has shown me from long experience and study of God's revelation in the scriptures.

After further thought, I decided to broaden this message to other relatives, both on my side of the family and on the side of my wife, Judy, my bride of over fifty years. After adding these groups together, I came up with dozens of people—younger, middle aged, older, girls, boys, women, men—for whom I care much. So many cousins, nieces, and nephews—some with children and grandchildren of their own—are frequently on my mind and in my prayers, even though it has been years since I have seen some of them.

Finally, I determined to write this for anyone and everyone who is looking for, or seeking to develop, answers to life's biggest questions: the things that matter most. I do not want to leave this world without briefly putting these thoughts down, without sharing what I believe are the essential matters of life and death. One who finds the water of life wants to tell everyone about it, especially those who are most thirsty. This was the experience of the woman at the well with Jesus, recorded in the fourth chapter of John's gospel, and it has been my experience for over a half century.

The Motive. I am writing out of love, which I define as the seeking of another's highest good, when good is determined by the teachings in God's Word, the Bible. The word love is mostly used in today's culture to signify a feeling. For a great many people, the emotional element is far more important than the factual, logical aspects of the issue at hand. The word love can and does mean anything the speaker wants it to mean. Usually the speaker has never attempted to define the word, so it floats around quite lacking in substance. What we commonly hear, nonetheless, is that love is all that matters.

Understood correctly, this last statement is the supreme truth of the universe. I trust that my love as expressed here will flow from the mind and heart of the God who is love (1 John 4:8)—the

My Credo

One who unfailingly seeks the highest good of every person on earth, as he alone determines our good, according to his all-wise and all-gracious purposes, in both this life and the life to come.

I am trying to write as simply as possible (but not simplistically, I trust). I have earned bachelor's, master's, and PhD degrees in biblical studies and theology, and have published at both the academic and the popular levels, and have taught for twenty-five years in three colleges and graduate schools. Yet I am basically an ordinary person with a desire for simplicity in my life and clarity in my thoughts, words, and actions. Following are the things that matter most to me—the key elements of my credo.

1. *I believe* that there is such a thing as objective truth, and that we can and must know it in order to survive and flourish.

   "Then you will know the truth, and the truth will set you free" (John 8:32). "Buy the truth and do not sell it—wisdom, instruction, and insight as well" (Prov 23:23).

2. *I believe* that God—Father, Son, and Spirit—is the ultimate truth, and that he longs to reveal himself to all people.

   "I [Jesus] am the way and the truth and the life. No one comes to the Father except through me" (John 14:6). "This is good, and pleases God our Savior, who wants all people to be saved and to come to a knowledge of the truth" (1 Tim 2:4).

3. *I believe* that God's truth is understood not only—nor even primarily—by human reasoning, but by spiritual insight, as we respond in trust and obedience to the truth we already know.

   "When I [the Apostle Paul] came to you, I did not come with eloquence or human wisdom as I proclaimed to you the testimony about God.... My message and my preaching were not with wise and persuasive words, but with a demonstration of the Spirit's power, so that your faith might not rest on human wisdom, but on God's power" (1 Cor 2:1–5). "Anyone who chooses to do the will of God will find out whether my teaching comes from God or whether I speak on my own" (John 7:17).

Appendix

4. *I believe* that the most important decision a person will ever make—the decision (or series of decisions) that will determine the quality of their life here on earth and throughout eternity—is whether or not they will respond with yes to the call of God to receive Jesus Christ as their Savior and Master. I believe that this call of God is both a gracious invitation and a non-negotiable command. Salvation cannot be earned; it is the gift of God's free grace received when a person responds to God's call, with trust in his promises, and through submission to the lordship of Christ.

    "Repent, then, and turn to God, so that your sins may be wiped out, that times of refreshing may come from the Lord, and that he may send the Messiah, who has been appointed for you—even Jesus" (Acts 3:19–20). "Very truly I [Jesus] tell you, no one can see the kingdom of God unless they are born again" (John 3:3).

5. *I believe* that those who are not able to make a decision for Christ because they are too young, too mentally disabled, or too ignorant of the gospel, are not forgotten by God. They are being drawn by him toward the truth according to his mysterious will and personal knowledge of each person. I also believe that anyone who has ever been saved, or ever will be saved, receives the gift of life because of the redeeming work of Jesus on the cross.

    "The true light [Jesus Christ] that gives light to everyone was coming into the world" (John 1:9). "And I, [Jesus], when I am lifted up from the earth, will draw all people to myself. . . . I am the way and the truth and the life. No one comes to the Father except through me" (John 12:32; 14:6). "Will not the Judge of all the earth do right?" (Gen 18:25).

6. *I believe* that the message of Jesus Christ is the only true and lasting hope for every person and every world crisis, and that this gospel must be taught and lived everywhere in obedience to Christ.

My Credo

"Therefore go and make disciples of all nations, baptizing them in the name of the Father and of the Son and of the Holy Spirit, and teaching them to obey everything I have commanded you. And surely I am with you always, to the very end of the age" (Matt 28:19-20). "For I [Paul] am not ashamed of the gospel, because it is the power of God that brings salvation to everyone who believes; first to the Jew, then to the Gentile" (Rom 1:16).

7. *I believe* that once a person comes to know God personally, they will grow and flourish in their new life only through Christian fellowship, study of the scriptures, and prayer—the latter two being both in private and with others.

    "Seven times a day I praise you for your righteous laws. Great peace have those who love your law, and nothing can make them stumble" (Ps 119:164-65). "And let us consider how we may spur one another on toward love and good deeds, not giving up meeting together, as some are in the habit of doing, but encouraging one another—and all the more as you see the Day approaching" (Heb 10:24-25).

8. *I believe* that the Bible is the inspired and infallible Word of God, given to everyone as the final authority for our knowledge of God and his will for our lives.

    "[From infancy you, Timothy,] have known the Holy Scriptures, which are able to make you wise for salvation through faith in Jesus Christ. All Scripture is God-breathed and is useful for teaching, rebuking, correction and training in righteousness, so that the servant of God may be thoroughly equipped for every good work" (2 Tim 3:15-17). "How sweet are your words to my taste, sweeter than honey to my mouth" (Ps 119:103).

9. *I believe* that the best prayer life consists of special times alone with God, times with others, and—perhaps most important of all—moment-by-moment communion with God throughout the day during which one utters, even if briefly,

Appendix

words of joy, worship, thanksgiving, confession, frustration, discouragement, request, and hope.

"Rejoice always, pray continually, give thanks in all circumstances; for this is God's will for you in Christ Jesus" (1 Thess 5:16-18). "But you, dear friends, by building yourselves up in your most holy faith and praying in the Holy Spirit, keep yourselves in God's love as you wait for the mercy of our Lord Jesus Christ to bring you to eternal life" (Jude 20-21).

10. *I believe* that sin is never to be treated lightly or joked about, but is to be recognized for what it is: the destroyer of our peace and joy, the destroyer of world peace and happiness, the destroyer of all things good and noble, and (if not confessed to God) the destroyer of our souls.

    "But among you there must not be even a hint of sexual immorality, or of any kind of impurity, or of greed, because these are improper for God's holy people. Nor should there be obscenity, foolish talk or coarse joking, which are out of place, but rather thanksgiving. For of this you can be sure: No immoral, impure or greedy person—such a person is an idolater—has any inheritance in the kingdom of Christ and of God" (Eph 5:3-5). "Very truly I [Jesus] tell you, everyone who sins is a slave to sin. . . . [But] if the Son sets you free, you will be free indeed" (John 8:34, 36).

11. *I believe* that the areas of self-love, money, sex, and power are some of the most crucial dimensions of our existence. Our responses in these areas will almost certainly determine the direction of our entire lives. I also believe that God is able and willing to break bondages in these and all other areas when we admit that we are powerless to deliver ourselves, and acknowledge that God is supremely powerful to rescue and establish us, even as he works patiently through those he has gifted to walk with us in the journey of life.

    "There will be terrible times in the last days. People will be lovers of themselves, lovers of money, boastful, proud, abusive, disobedient to their parents, ungrateful, unholy,

My Credo

without love, unforgiving, slanderous, without self-control, brutal, not lovers of the good, treacherous, rash, conceited, lovers of pleasure rather than lovers of God—having a form of godliness but denying its power" (2 Tim 3:1–5). "And that is what some of you were. But you were washed, you were sanctified, you were justified in the name of the Lord Jesus Christ and by the Spirit of our God" (1 Cor 6:11).

12. *I believe* that, no matter how many people try to deny or escape from this truth, there will be a solemn Day of Judgment following our death, at which everyone will be assigned to their eternal destination based upon their reception or rejection of the truth they have been offered in this life.

    "Then I [John] saw a great white throne and him who was seated on it. . . . And I saw the dead, great and small, standing before the throne, and books were opened. Another book was opened, which is the book of life. The dead were judged according to what they had done as recorded in the books. . . . Anyone whose name was not found written in the book of life was thrown into the lake of fire" (Rev 20:11–12, 15). "They perish because they refused to love the truth and so be saved. For this reason God sends them a powerful delusion so that they will believe the lie and so that all will be condemned who have not believed the truth but have delighted in wickedness" (2 Thess 2:10–12).

13. *I believe* that every child of God should be involved in a healthy local church—one where the leaders are humble servants of God, the scriptures are preached in the wisdom and power of the Spirit, the worship is focused on God, not ourselves; where the worshippers exude true love for one another and for outsiders, and where there are no barriers between, or preferential treatment toward, men or women, young or old, one racial group or another, one educational level or another, nor one social class above another.

    "After this I [John] looked, and there before me was a great multitude that no one could count, from every nation,

Appendix

tribe, people and language, standing before the throne and before the Lamb. They were wearing white robes and were holding palm branches in their hands" (Rev 7:9). "There is neither Jew nor Gentile, neither slave nor free, nor is there male and female, for you are all one in Christ Jesus" (Gal 3:28).

14. *I believe* that no child of God ever needs to compromise his or her God-given convictions in order to obtain the necessities of life: housing, food, clothing, a job, or personal safety. God may allow us to suffer deprivation in one or more of these areas for a time, but he will never remove his loving eye and care from those who faithfully trust and obey him.

    "[Seek] first his [God's] kingdom and his righteousness, and all these things [food, clothing, security] will be given to you as well" (Matt 6:33). "Cast your cares on the LORD and he will sustain you; he will never let the righteous be shaken" (Ps 55:22). "I would rather be a doorkeeper in the house of my God than dwell in the tents of the wicked" (Ps 84:10). "And my God will meet all your needs according to the riches of his glory in Christ Jesus" (Phil 4:19).

15. *I believe* that it is every Christian's privilege and responsibility to give liberally of their time, skills, energy, and financial resources toward alleviating the sufferings of this world, both the physical needs and the social, psychological, and spiritual deprivations that often lie behind the physical.

    "He has shown you, O mortal, what is good. And what does the Lord require of you? To act justly and to love mercy and to walk humbly with your God" (Mic 6:8). "Religion that God our Father accepts as pure and faultless is this: to look after orphans and widows in their distress and to keep oneself from being polluted by the world" (Jas 1:27). "Therefore, as we have opportunity, let us do good to all people, especially to those who belong to the family of believers" (Gal 6:10).

16. *I believe* that our best efforts to improve society and the lives of people everywhere, however well-intentioned, will result at best in only partial success, for two reasons. First, workable

My Credo

solutions depend heavily on the free choices of people to cooperate, which choices we cannot force. And second, workable solutions to society's most common problems (such as hunger, poor housing, theft, violence, racism, sexism, corruption of leaders, joblessness, addictions, poor education, and broken families) must be based on spiritual foundations that acknowledge both our pervasive human sinfulness—humans are not naturally good—and God's ever-reaching offers of grace and mercy. Human solutions apart from God's provisions will never adequately meet the deepest needs of our bodies, souls, communities, and nations.

"The heart is deceitful above all things and beyond cure. Who can understand it?" (Jer 17:9). "There is no difference between Jew and Gentile, for all have sinned and fall short of the glory of God, and all are justified freely by his grace through the redemption that came by Christ Jesus" (Rom 3:22–24). "If you do away with the yoke of oppression, with the pointing finger and malicious talk, and if you spend yourselves in behalf of the hungry and satisfy the needs of the oppressed, then your light will rise in the darkness, and your night will become like the noonday. The LORD will guide you always . . . then you will find your joy in the LORD" (Isa 58:9–11, 14).

17. *I believe* that there is an evil power in the world who, with God's permission, rules over this world system known as the cosmos. This one, called Satan or the devil, is also referred to (by Jesus) as the prince of this world (John 12:31) and (by Paul) as the god of this age (2 Cor 4:4). This evil one is, I believe, active in certain governmental, financial, educational, religious, and social systems, so much so that "the whole world is under the control of the evil one" (1 John 5:19). Our confidence, however, is firm, because "the one who is in you is greater than the one who is in the world" (1 John 4:4).

"I am Jesus . . . I am sending you [Paul] to them [unbelievers] to open their eyes and turn them from darkness to light and from the power of Satan to God, so that they

Appendix

may receive forgiveness of sins and a place among those who are sanctified by faith in me" (Acts 26:15–18). "Put on the full armor of God, so that you can take your stand against the devil's schemes. For our struggle is not against flesh and blood, but against the rulers, against the authorities, against the powers of this dark world and against the spiritual forces of evil in the heavenly realms" (Eph 6:11–12). "For though we live in the world, we do not wage war as the world does. The weapons we fight with are not the weapons of the world. On the contrary, they have divine power to demolish strongholds" (2 Cor 10:3–4).

18. *I believe* that one of the most effective weapons, if not the most effective, that the evil one uses against Christ's followers is to remind and accuse believers of their past sins—both old and new—that have been forgiven by God and cleansed by Christ's blood. While we are flawed in ourselves, we are his forgiven and cherished people, clothed in his righteousness. We must not allow the accusations of the devil (the word means "accuser") to block our peace, joy, and hope of being used mightily for God's purposes in the days and years ahead.

    "The great dragon was hurled down—that ancient serpent called the devil, or Satan, who leads the whole world astray. . . . For the accuser of our brothers and sisters, who accuses them before our God day and night, has been hurled down. They triumphed over him by the blood of the Lamb and the word of their testimony; they did not love their lives so much as to shrink from death" (Rev 12:9–11). "What, then, shall we say in response to these things? If God is for us, who can be against us? . . . Who will bring any charge against those whom God has chosen? It is God who justifies. Who then is the one who condemns? No one" (Rom 8:31–34).

19. *I believe* that one essential prayer for every believer to express often is to ask God to examine and reveal to us our inner thoughts and motives. This is important because we are all pulled subtly toward dishonesty, self-deception, and

My Credo

self-justification, unless we regularly open the windows of our soul to the light of God's truth.

"Search me, God, and know my heart; test me and know my anxious thoughts. See if there is any offensive way in me, and lead me in the way everlasting" (Ps 139: 23–24). "[Who] can discern their own errors? Forgive my hidden faults. . . . May these words of my mouth and this meditation of my heart be pleasing in your sight, LORD, my Rock and my Redeemer" (Ps 19:12, 14).

20. *I believe* that God's kingdom is an upside-down kingdom, where the things most highly esteemed and celebrated by the world are often the opposite of what God prizes and praises. Conversely, the things most looked down upon in the eyes of the world are often the most highly regarded in the eyes of God.

"What people value highly," [said Jesus], "is detestable in God's sight" (Luke 16:15). "Believers in humble circumstances ought to take pride in their high position. But the rich should take pride in their humiliation—since they will pass away like a wild flower" (Jas 1:9–10). "For the foolishness of God is wiser than human wisdom, and the weakness of God is stronger than human strength" (1 Cor 1:25). "My grace is sufficient for you, [says the Lord,] for my power is made perfect in weakness. . . . That is why, for Christ's sake, I [Paul] delight in weaknesses, in insults, in hardships, in persecutions, in difficulties. For when I am weak, then I am strong" (2 Cor 12:9–10).

21. *I believe* that there is not a single command from God that he will not give us the power to obey if we admit our helplessness apart from him, and then boldly step forward in faith (trust) that he is now working in us according to his perfect will.

"Let us then approach God's throne of grace with confidence, so that we may receive mercy and find grace to help us in our time of need" (Heb 4:16). "No temptation [or test] has overtaken you except what is common to mankind. And

Appendix

God is faithful; he will not let you be tempted beyond what you can bear. But when you are temped, he will also provide a way out so that you can endure it" (1 Cor 10:13). "I [Paul] can do all things through him [the Lord] who gives me strength" (Phil 4:13).

22. *I believe* that the Lord's Prayer, while not intended by Jesus to serve as a rigid prayer formula for us, is the most remarkable and powerful prayer in the Bible. It is from the perfect God-man himself. Jesus said that this is how we should pray. It covers the most important areas of the believer's life. I believe that every time we pray this prayer, slowly and sincerely, thinking deeply about each part, we will experience the closeness and goodness of God and God's answers to our longings.

    "Our Father in heaven, hallowed be your name, your kingdom come, your will be done, on earth as it is in heaven. Give us today our daily bread. And forgive us our debts, as we also have forgiven our debtors. And lead us not into temptation, but deliver us from the evil one" (Matt 6:9–13).

23. *I believe* that the wisest, happiest, and most helpful people are those who walk closely with God throughout their days, knowing that they are forgiven and blessed children of the Lord almighty, and are being guided by his loving hand through the highs and lows of their earthly journey.

    "Jesus stood and said in a loud voice, 'Let anyone who is thirsty come to me and drink. Whoever believes in me, as Scripture has said, rivers of living water will flow from within them'" (John 7:37–38). "Though you have not seen him [Jesus Christ], you love him; and even though you do not see him now, you believe in him and are filled with an inexpressible and glorious joy, for you are receiving the end result of your faith, the salvation of your souls" (1 Pet 1:8–9).

24. *I believe* that everyone reading this message, regardless of how you have lived or are now living, is very special in the eyes of God. You have been created in his image, for his glory and your eternal happiness. You are the product of your

My Credo

nature (genetics), nurture (upbringing), and life-experiences (many of which were beyond your control), but you are also where and who you are because of your choices. Regardless of whether your choices to this point have been wise or unwise, godly or ungodly, your future is now wide open—for this life and the life to come. I believe that you can, right now, by the mighty grace of God strengthening your will, enter the life that God has designed for you. Whether you are a long-time believer, new believer, backslidden believer, nonbeliever, or not even sure, I urge you to come to God today, with faith and humility as a little child. Talk to him as you would to your best friend. He will never reject you.

"We [Paul and his associates] implore you on Christ's behalf: be reconciled to God. God made him who had no sin to be sin for us, so that in him we might become the righteousness of God. As God's coworkers we urge you not to receive God's grace in vain. . . . I tell you, now is the day of salvation" (2 Cor 5:20—6:2). "'For I know the plans I have for you,' declares the LORD, 'plans to prosper you and not to harm you, plans to give you hope and a future. Then you will call on me and come and pray to me, and I will listen to you. You will seek me and find me when you seek me with all your heart. I will be found by you,' declares the LORD, 'and will bring you back from captivity'" (Jer 29:11-14).

This, my credo, is a brief summary of what I believe. I encourage you, good reader, to develop your own credo. It may not be easy, but it will surely benefit you, especially if you have your Bible open as you write. I trust that this message, written in love, will nourish your soul deeply. God bless you always as you flourish in his truth and love.

Bibliography

Alcorn, Randy. *Heaven*. Wheaton: Tyndale, 2004.
———. *If God Is Good: Faith in the Midst of Suffering and Evil*. Colorado Springs, CO: Multnomah, 2009.
Blomberg, Craig. *Can We Still Believe in God?* Grand Rapids: Brazos, 2020.
Bonar, Andrew. *Robert Murray M'Cheyne: Memoir and Remains*. Edinburgh: Banner of Truth Trust, 1966.
Bridge, Donald, and David Phypers. *The Water that Divides*. Downers Grove: InterVarsity, 1977.
Carson, Donald A. *Collected Writings on Scripture*, compiled by Andrew D. Naselli. Wheaton: Crossway, 2010.
———. *How Long, O Lord? Reflections on Suffering and Evil*. 2nd ed. Grand Rapids: Baker, 2006.
———. *Matthew*. Expositor's Bible Commentary series, vol. 10. Grand Rapids: Zondervan, 1984.
Carter, Tom, comp. *2200 Quotations from the Writings of Charles H. Spurgeon*. Grand Rapids: Baker, 1988.
Crockett, William, ed. *Four Views on Hell*. Grand Rapids: Zondervan, 1992.
Edwards, David, and John Stott. *Evangelical Essentials: A Liberal-Evangelical Dialogue*. Downers Grove: InterVarsity, 1989.
Erickson, Millard J. *Christian Theology*. 2nd ed. Grand Rapids: Baker, 1998.
Gilmore, John. *Probing Heaven: Key Questions on the Hereafter*. Grand Rapids: Baker, 1989.
Grenz, Stanley J. *Theology for the Community of God*. Grand Rapids: Eerdmans, 2000.
Grudem, Wayne. *Systematic Theology*. Zondervan, 1994.

Bibliography

Hallesby, O. *Infant Baptism and Adult Conversion*. Minneapolis: Augsburg, 1924.

———. *Why I Am a Christian*. Minneapolis: Augsburg, 1930.

Helm, Paul. "Faith, Evidence, and the Scriptures." In *Scripture and Truth*, edited by D. Carson and J. Woodbridge, 299–320. Grand Rapids: Zondervan, 1983.

Jeschke, Marlin. *Believers Baptism for Children of the Church*. Eugene, OR: Wipf and Stock, 2000.

Laidlaw, Robert A. *The Reasons Why*. Grand Rapids: Zondervan, 1970.

Lewis, C. S. *Mere Christianity*. New York: Macmillan, 1952.

Rakestraw, Robert V. *GraceQuest: One Teacher's Relentless Pursuit of Salvation, Spirituality and the Grace to Suffer Well*. Eugene, OR: Wipf and Stock, 2015.

Rakestraw, Robert, with Jane Spriggs. *Heart Cries: Praying by the Spirit in the Midst of Life*. N. p.: 2010.

Strobel, Lee. *The Case for Christ*. Grand Rapids: Zondervan, 1998.

———. *The Case for Faith*. Grand Rapids: Zondervan, 2000.

Strong, Augustus Hopkins. *Systematic Theology*. 3 vols. Philadelphia: Judson, 1907.

Toon, Peter. *Heaven and Hell: A Biblical and Theological Overview*. Nashville: Thomas Nelson, 1986.

Walls, Jerry L. *Heaven, Hell, and Purgatory: A Protestant View of the Cosmic Drama*. Grand Rapids: Brazos, 2015.

Wenham, John. *Christ and the Bible*. 2nd ed. Grand Rapids: Baker, 1984.

Wilkinson, Bruce. *A Life God Rewards*. Colorado Springs, CO: Multnomah, 2002.

Wright, N. T. *Surprised by Hope: Rethinking Heaven, the Resurrection, and the Mission of the Church*. San Francisco: Harper One, 2008.

www.ingramcontent.com/pod-product-compliance
Lightning Source LLC
Chambersburg PA
CBHW070927160426
43193CB00011B/1598